THE ECHO OF ETERNITY

UNLOCKING THE REVELATIONS OF RENEWAL AND PURPOSE

Tina Ketch

THE ECHO OF ETERNITY
UNLOCKING THE REVELATIONS OF RENEWAL AND PURPOSE

TinaKetch.com

ISBN: 979-8-9921669-8-9
eISBN: 979-8-9921669-9-6

First Edition: January 2025

FOREWORD

The Book of Revelation is one of the most compelling and enigmatic texts in the Bible. Its vivid imagery, powerful symbols, and apocalyptic visions have intrigued readers and scholars for centuries. Yet, beyond its mystery lies a timeless invitation—a call to explore the depths of divine truth, to awaken to our spiritual potential, and to engage in the sacred work of renewal.

This book is a guide to navigating Revelation's rich tapestry of meanings and its relevance in our modern world. In its pages, the author masterfully bridges ancient wisdom with contemporary challenges, showing us how Revelation's teachings speak to our deepest personal struggles and the collective trials we face as humanity.

What makes this work particularly profound is its ability to shift our perspective. Revelation has often been seen as a book of fear, filled with foreboding warnings of judgment and destruction. But here, it becomes a text of hope—a testament to resilience, transformation, and divine love. The author reveals how its visions of the New Jerusalem, the Tree of Life, and the River of Life are not distant promises but living realities that we are called to embody in our daily lives.

The journey through this book is both introspective and expansive. It challenges us to confront our inner barriers, embrace personal growth, and find strength in our faith. At the same time, it calls us to act collectively, addressing social injustices, environmental crises, and divisions within our communities. The blending of personal and collective transformation reflects the heart of Revelation's message: that we are all interconnected, and our shared destiny is one of renewal and unity.

What sets this book apart is its inclusivity. It draws on a wealth of traditions, linking Revelation to the seven chakras, mystical interpretations, and cross-cultural insights that enrich our understanding. This integration of Eastern and Western spiritual wisdom highlights the universality of Revelation's call. Whether you are a Christian seeking deeper meaning, a spiritual seeker exploring new perspectives, or simply someone yearning for hope in challenging times, this book speaks to you.

As you delve into its chapters, you will find yourself reflecting on profound questions:

- How do Revelation's symbols relate to my own journey of faith and transformation?
- What does it mean to live in alignment with the principles of justice, love, and renewal?
- How can I contribute to the collective vision of the New Jerusalem—a world of harmony, compassion, and divine unity?

This book does not offer easy answers or shy away from the complexities of Revelation. Instead, it invites you into a dialogue with the text, encouraging you to wrestle with its meanings and discover its relevance in your own life. It provides tools for personal reflection, meditative practices, and actionable steps for engaging with the world in meaningful ways.

I am confident that as you read, you will find yourself inspired—not only by the beauty of Revelation's imagery but by its enduring power to guide us toward transformation. The author's insights and passion for this subject illuminate the path, making this book a companion for anyone seeking to live with purpose, courage, and faith.

Revelation reminds us that even amidst chaos and uncertainty, the light of hope endures. This book reminds us that this light is not only something to be found—it is something to be lived, shared, and nurtured in ourselves and others.

May this journey bring you closer to the divine vision of unity and renewal that Revelation promises. May it challenge and inspire you to grow, to act, and to believe in the eternal promise of restoration and peace.

PREFACE

A Journey Into Revelation's Timeless Wisdom

The Book of Revelation stands as one of the most enigmatic and awe-inspiring texts in the Bible. Its vivid imagery, apocalyptic visions, and profound prophecies have inspired centuries of reflection, debate, and interpretation. Yet beyond its mystique lies a deeper truth: Revelation is not merely a book about endings; it is a guide to transformation, hope, and renewal.

This book invites us to see Revelation in a new light—not as a foreboding account of doom but as a living testament to humanity's potential for spiritual growth and collective harmony. It challenges us to look beyond its symbols of judgment and tribulation to discover its enduring lessons for navigating the complexities of our modern world.

As we face global challenges such as environmental crises, social inequality, and political instability, Revelation's message resonates more than ever. It urges us to confront fear with faith, to overcome adversity with resilience, and to embrace renewal with hope. Its visions of the New Jerusalem and the Tree of Life remind us that transformation is always possible, even in the face of uncertainty.

In this book, we explore Revelation not as a standalone text but as a bridge between ancient wisdom and contemporary action. We delve into its profound connections with other scriptures, its alignment with mystical traditions, and its relevance to the pressing issues of our time. We draw insights from its symbols, such as the Seven Seals and the 144,000, uncovering their spiritual and practical significance.

This journey through Revelation is both personal and collective. It invites each of us to embark on an inward path of self-discovery while also calling us to work together in building a world grounded in justice, love, and unity. Whether you are seeking spiritual awakening, practical guidance, or a deeper understanding of Revelation's mysteries, this book offers a framework for applying its timeless truths to your life.

The chapters ahead are not just an exploration—they are a call to action. They challenge us to integrate Revelation's teachings into our daily lives, transforming its visions into reality. Each page is an opportunity to reflect, grow, and engage with the sacred work of renewal.

As you begin this journey, I encourage you to approach Revelation with an open heart and a willingness to see its teachings in a new way. May its wisdom inspire you to live with purpose, act with compassion, and trust in the promise of divine restoration.

Let us walk this path together, discovering the beauty, depth, and transformative power of Revelation—a message as eternal as the light it promises.

Tina Ketch

PROLOGUE

The Echo of Eternity

In a quiet village perched at the edge of a vast desert, there stood a library untouched by time. At its heart was a single, ancient book bound in worn leather. It bore no title on its cover, only an embossed image of an open door. Few dared to touch it, for legends spoke of its contents as both terrifying and transformative. The villagers called it *The Echo of Eternity.*

One evening, a traveler arrived—a seeker of truth named Elias. Weathered by years of wandering, he entered the library, drawn inexplicably to the mysterious book. He asked the librarian, a wise woman with eyes like deep wells, about the book's purpose.

"It is not a book to be read lightly," she warned. "It speaks of endings and beginnings, chaos and order, despair and hope. It is a mirror and a map. Many leave it more confused than when they began, but a few—" she paused, her gaze piercing—"a few find clarity that changes everything."

Intrigued, Elias opened the book. Its first words struck him like a thunderclap: *"Blessed are those who hear these words and take them to heart."*

The pages unfolded a vision—a symphony of symbols, a dance of beasts and angels, a descent into shadows, and an ascent into light. At first, Elias was overwhelmed. The dragon seemed too fierce, the plagues too cruel, the battles too endless. But as he read, he began to see patterns emerge. The chaos was not meaningless; it was a purging fire, stripping away falsehood to reveal the truth.

Elias discovered that the book was not a tale of destruction but of renewal. It whispered to him that endings were not punishments but thresholds, and behind the fearsome imagery lay profound truths: unity could rise from division, love could conquer hatred, and life could triumph over death. The New Jerusalem was not merely a city; it was a state of being—a promise of harmony for those who dared to hope.

Yet the book did more than speak to him—it spoke through him. The words etched themselves into his soul, illuminating his own struggles, choices, and purpose. He realized that the beasts were not only external forces but reflections of inner fears. The angels were not distant beings but echoes of his higher self. Revelation was not merely a prophecy of the future but a guide for the present—a call to align one's life with truth and grace.

As he closed the book, Elias felt transformed. The librarian smiled knowingly.

"You see now," she said, "why this book must be read with both reverence and courage. It is not only the story of the world but the story of every soul. It challenges you to believe—not in the impossible, but in the inevitable victory of love and renewal. It asks you to understand—not to fear the end but to embrace it as the doorway to something greater. And it beckons you to read—not just for knowledge, but for the wisdom to live with purpose."

Elias left the library that night, carrying no book in his hand but its truths in his heart. He walked into the desert not as a wanderer but as a pilgrim, knowing that every step brought him closer to the New Jerusalem—not in some distant realm but within himself.

Why Read the Book?

The Echo of Eternity—or Revelation—is not just a collection of visions; it is a call to awaken. It invites the reader to see beyond the surface of their fears and struggles, to understand the profound cycles of life, death, and renewal, and to believe in the enduring power of grace and love. It is a book that challenges, heals, and transforms, offering a vision of hope that can inspire humanity to live with courage, unity, and purpose.

Revelation is not merely a book to be studied; it is a journey to be lived. It is the whisper of eternity calling you home. Will you answer?

DEDICATION

To you, the reader—

This book is for the seeker who asks, "What lies beyond?" It is for the dreamer who envisions a better world and for the believer who holds fast to the promise of hope, even in the face of uncertainty. It is for those who long to uncover the deeper truths that bind us together and connect us to the divine.

You are the reason these words have been written. Your courage to question, reflect, and transform is a testament to the infinite potential of the human spirit. You are part of a greater journey, one that spans generations and touches every corner of existence—a journey of renewal, justice, and unity.

This book is dedicated to the moments when you have stood at the crossroads of doubt and faith and chosen to move forward. It is for the times you've faced fear with resilience, answered hatred with love, and sought understanding when division seemed inevitable. It honors your commitment to live authentically, to grow spiritually, and to embrace the sacred calling to co-create a world of compassion and harmony.

May these pages be a source of inspiration, encouragement, and strength as you walk your unique path. May they challenge you to see Revelation not as an abstract vision, but as a living guide—a beacon of light in the complexities of our modern age.

To the individual reading these words, know that you are not alone. You are part of a greater story, one that calls each of us to rise above fear, to reach out in love, and to build bridges of understanding in a world yearning for connection.

Thank you for your openness, curiosity, and willingness to engage with the eternal truths that bind us to one another and to the divine. Your journey matters, your contributions matter, and your presence in this sacred story of life and renewal is invaluable.

With heartfelt gratitude and hope for the road ahead,

Tina

TABLE OF CONTENTS

INTRODUCTION

Revelation's Living Legacy

How to Read Revelation: A Step-by-Step Guide

Revelation is one of the most enigmatic books of the Bible, filled with vivid symbols, prophetic visions, and powerful messages. Understanding how to approach it can transform confusion into clarity and fear into inspiration. This guide provides practical steps to help readers unlock its profound insights:

1. Understand the Genre of Revelation

Revelation is apocalyptic literature, a genre that uses symbolic language, visions, and metaphors to convey divine truths. It's not meant to be read as a literal narrative but as a spiritual and symbolic map of humanity's journey.

- **Why This Matters**: Knowing the genre prevents misinterpretation. Symbols like the Beast, the Lamb, or the Seven Seals are not meant to be taken literally but as representations of spiritual and societal realities.
- **Tip**: Approach the text with curiosity and openness, seeking the deeper meanings behind the imagery.

2. Contextual Reading: Historical and Cultural Background

Revelation was written during a time of Roman persecution against Christians. Understanding this context illuminates its urgency and relevance.

- **Why This Matters**: Knowing the struggles of early Christians helps modern readers connect with the book's themes of endurance, faith, and hope.

- **Tip**: Research the Roman Imperial Cult, the destruction of the Temple in Jerusalem, and the early Christian experience to better understand the text's background.

3. Symbolic vs. Literal Interpretation

Many of Revelation's visions are symbolic rather than literal depictions of future events. Recognizing this helps uncover the spiritual truths within.

- **Why This Matters**: A symbolic interpretation allows for broader, timeless applications, whereas a literal reading can lead to fear or confusion.
- **Tip**: Focus on the essence of each symbol. For example, the New Jerusalem represents unity and restoration rather than a physical city.

4. Personal and Collective Relevance

Revelation speaks to both personal spiritual growth and collective transformation.

- **Why This Matters**: It highlights the interconnectedness of individual choices and societal shifts.
- **Tip**: Reflect on how its lessons apply to your own life and community, particularly its themes of justice, renewal, and perseverance.

5. Practical Tips for Engaging with Revelation

- **Daily Reflections**: Begin each reading session with a moment of prayer or meditation, asking for guidance in understanding the text.
- **Journaling**: Write down insights, questions, and personal connections to Revelation's teachings.

- **Group Discussions**: Join or form a study group to explore Revelation collaboratively, benefiting from diverse perspectives.
- **Supplemental Resources**: Use commentaries, historical studies, or guided reflections to deepen your understanding.

6. Embrace the Journey of Revelation

Reading Revelation is not about finding definitive answers but about engaging with its profound questions and truths. It invites readers to embark on a journey of faith, hope, and transformation.

- **Why This Matters**: Revelation is a living text, speaking to each generation in unique ways.
- **Tip**: Let its messages inspire you to live with purpose and align your actions with divine principles.

By following this guide, readers can approach Revelation with confidence and curiosity, unlocking its timeless wisdom and applying it meaningfully to their lives.

The Book of Revelation is a testament to the enduring power of divine revelation. For centuries, its vivid imagery and profound messages have sparked reflection, debate, and transformation among readers. Often misunderstood as a harbinger of destruction, Revelation is, in fact, a guide to renewal, resilience, and hope. It bridges the temporal and the eternal, calling individuals and communities to rise above fear and align with divine purpose.

Written in a time of turmoil and persecution, Revelation offered early Christians not only comfort but also a blueprint for spiritual fortitude. Today, its lessons remain relevant, challenging us to find meaning and courage in the face of our own struggles. Its intricate symbols—the Lamb, the Seven Seals, the Four Horsemen, and the New Jerusalem—resonate as timeless archetypes of humanity's journey toward unity, justice, and peace.

This journey through Revelation will take us across three dimensions: the historical past, the dynamic present, and the aspirational future. By exploring its spiritual depths, we can uncover practical applications for our lives and communities. Together, we will embark on a path of understanding and action, discovering how Revelation continues to illuminate our personal and collective transformations. In this journey, we will explore Revelation's teachings as a living guide that bridges the past, present, and future. Each part of this exploration unveils new ways to connect with its eternal message, enabling us to carry its light into every aspect of our lives.

Introduction: Revelation's Living Legacy

The Book of Revelation is a testament to the enduring power of divine revelation. For centuries, its vivid imagery and profound messages have sparked reflection, debate, and transformation among readers. Often misunderstood as a harbinger of destruction, Revelation is, in fact, a guide to renewal, resilience, and hope. It bridges the temporal and the eternal, calling individuals and communities to rise above fear and align with divine purpose.

Written during a time of turmoil and persecution, Revelation offered early Christians not only comfort but also a blueprint for spiritual fortitude. Today, its lessons remain relevant, challenging us to find meaning and courage in the face of our own struggles. Its intricate symbols—the Lamb, the Seven Seals, the Four Horsemen, and the New Jerusalem—resonate as timeless archetypes of humanity's journey toward unity, justice, and peace.

This journey through Revelation will take us across three dimensions: the historical past, the dynamic present, and the aspirational future. By exploring its spiritual depths, we can uncover practical applications for our lives and communities. Together, we will embark on a path of understanding and action, discovering how Revelation continues to illuminate our personal and collective transformations. In this journey, we will explore Revelation's teachings as a living guide that bridges the past, present, and future. Each part of this exploration unveils new ways to connect with its eternal message, enabling us to carry its light into every aspect of our lives.

PART ONE

UNDERSTANDING REVELATION'S HISTORICAL CONTEXT

Revelation emerged during a time of immense persecution for early Christians under Roman rule. The oppressive regime sought to enforce emperor worship through the Roman Imperial Cult, where refusing to venerate the emperor as a deity often meant facing dire consequences. This tension between faith and authority formed the backdrop for Revelation's urgent and hope-filled message, written to encourage believers to stand firm in their convictions.

The Seven Churches: A Mirror of Human Struggles

The Seven Churches addressed in Revelation's opening chapters illustrate the diverse challenges early Christians faced. These letters, while contextual, are timeless in their reflection of spiritual struggles:

- **Ephesus**: This church was praised for its diligence and doctrinal purity but warned against losing its first love. This reflects a common spiritual challenge: maintaining passion and purpose amidst routine and obligation.
- **Smyrna**: Commended for enduring poverty and persecution, the believers in Smyrna exemplified how spiritual richness can coexist with material lack. Their faith serves as a reminder of the enduring power of hope during hardship.
- **Pergamum**: This church struggled with compromise, facing external pressures to conform to cultural norms. Their situation resonates today as a call to hold firm to one's values amidst societal opposition.
- **Laodicea**: Criticized for being lukewarm, the believers in Laodicea were called to reignite their faith. Their story speaks to

the danger of complacency and the importance of spiritual renewal.

Each of these letters is a microcosm of the broader themes of Revelation: perseverance, repentance, and the promise of divine vindication.

Historical Events That Shaped Revelation

The historical context of Revelation profoundly influenced its imagery and message:

1. The Reign of Nero: Nero's brutal persecution of Christians, including the infamous martyrdoms in Rome, cast him as a figure of apocalyptic tyranny. This historical memory likely inspired the depiction of the Beast as a symbol of corrupt power.
2. The Destruction of the Temple (70 CE): The fall of the Second Temple in Jerusalem was a catastrophic event for the Jewish people, symbolizing judgment and exile. For Christians, it reinforced Revelation's themes of renewal, where destruction precedes restoration.
3. Roman Imperial Cult: The demand to worship the emperor placed Christians in a moral crisis, compelling them to choose between compliance and faithfulness. Revelation's call to resist such idolatry was a rallying cry for early believers to remain steadfast.

Revelation's Imagery: Strength in the Face of Adversity

Revelation's vivid symbols offered a way for Christians to interpret their suffering through a divine lens:

- **The Dragon and the Beast**: Representations of oppressive forces, these symbols reminded believers of the ultimate defeat of evil.

- **The Sealed Scroll**: A symbol of divine knowledge and purpose, the scroll reassured believers that their trials were part of a greater plan.
- **The White Robes**: Worn by the martyrs, these robes symbolized victory and purity, offering hope to those who endured persecution.

Timeless Lessons from the Past

The struggles of early Christians remind us that challenges, though painful, are opportunities for spiritual growth. Their courage and steadfastness inspire us to:

- **Stand Firm in Values**: Just as the early believers resisted the pressures of the Roman Empire, we are called to uphold our principles even in the face of societal opposition.
- **Find Hope in Adversity**: The letters to the Seven Churches remind us that every struggle is an opportunity for renewal and greater alignment with divine purpose.
- **Recognize the Bigger Picture**: Revelation teaches that our trials are part of a larger story of redemption and restoration.

By delving into Revelation's historical context, we connect with its enduring relevance. The challenges faced by early Christians are not unlike those we encounter today—pressures to conform, fears of uncertainty, and the temptation to lose sight of our purpose. Yet, Revelation reminds us that through faith, resilience, and the promise of divine renewal, we can navigate even the darkest times with hope and courage.

PART TWO

REVELATION'S SPIRITUAL SYMBOLS AND THEIR RELEVANCE

The symbols in Revelation are rich with spiritual meaning. They serve as timeless guides for navigating the complexities of human existence and spiritual growth. These symbols transcend historical confines, inviting each reader into a deeply personal journey of reflection and transformation.

The Lamb: Humility and Divine Love

The Lamb represents the ultimate symbol of humility, sacrifice, and divine love. In Revelation, the Lamb is depicted as the one worthy to open the sealed scroll, signifying a unique role in the divine plan. For early Christians, the Lamb symbolized Christ's selfless sacrifice, inspiring hope amid persecution.

In our lives, the Lamb calls us to:

- **Practice Compassion**: Extend kindness and understanding to others, even in challenging situations.
- **Embrace Humility**: Let go of ego and approach life with a spirit of service and gratitude.
- **Seek Redemption**: Recognize the power of forgiveness, both in seeking it and offering it to others.

The Lamb's role reminds us that transformative power often comes from gentleness and love, qualities that can shape our relationships and communities.

The Seven Seals: Stages of Spiritual Awakening

The Seven Seals represent transformative stages of spiritual awakening, each revealing deeper truths about humanity and the divine:

1. **The First Seal (White Horse)**: Symbolizing conquest, this horseman challenges us to examine our ambitions and their alignment with spiritual values.
2. **The Second Seal (Red Horse) Represents conflict and** prompts reflection on personal and collective sources of strife.
3. **The Third Seal (Black Horse)**: Associated with scarcity, it calls for mindfulness in our consumption and generosity toward others.
4. **The Fourth Seal (Pale Horse)**: Representing mortality, this seal reminds us of life's fragility and the importance of living purposefully.
5. **The Fifth Seal (Martyrs Under the Altar)**: Highlights the cost of steadfast faith and the eternal rewards of endurance.
6. **The Sixth Seal (Cosmic Disturbances)**: A vivid reminder of humanity's connection to the cosmos and the transformative power of divine intervention.
7. **The Seventh Seal (Silence in Heaven)**: Represents the stillness that precedes divine revelation, inviting us to embrace quiet moments for reflection.

As the seals are opened, they reveal a pathway to spiritual growth by confronting fear, materialism, and division.

The Four Horsemen: Trials That Refine the Soul

The Four Horsemen—often interpreted as harbingers of destruction—also serve as metaphors for the trials that refine our souls. Each horseman challenges us to rise above adversity:

- **The White Horse**: Calls us to examine our pursuits and align them with higher values.

- **The Red Horse**: Encourages peace-making and reconciliation in times of conflict.
- **The Black Horse**: Inspires us to reflect on fairness, equity, and the distribution of resources.
- **The Pale Horse**: Invites us to find meaning and strength in the face of life's inevitable challenges.

Through these symbols, Revelation teaches that our trials are not punishments but opportunities to strengthen our faith and deepen our understanding of divine purpose.

The New Jerusalem: Vision of Unity and Renewal

The New Jerusalem represents the culmination of Revelation's message—a vision of ultimate unity, peace, and renewal. This holy city descends as a symbol of divine reconciliation, where humanity and God dwell in harmony. Its descriptions—streets of gold, gates of pearl—are not mere adornments but representations of a world where justice and love prevail.

In our daily lives, the New Jerusalem inspires us to:

- **Build Inclusive Communities**: Create spaces where diversity is celebrated and everyone feels valued.
- **Promote Justice and Equity**: Work toward a society where fairness and compassion guide actions and policies.
- **Envision a Renewed Earth**: Care for the environment, reflecting the vision of a harmonious creation.

The New Jerusalem is not merely a destination but a blueprint for living in alignment with divine principles.

Unlocking Insights Through Meditation

To deepen our understanding of these symbols, consider the following meditative practices:

- **Reflect on the Lamb**: Visualize its gentleness and humility, asking how you can embody these qualities in your life.
- **Meditate on the Seals**: Contemplate which seal resonates with your current challenges and how its lessons can guide you.
- **Envision the New Jerusalem**: Imagine a world transformed by love, unity, and justice. Let this vision inspire your actions.

Practical Applications of Symbolism

Revelation's symbols are not confined to theological reflection; they offer practical insights for daily living:

- **Personal Growth**: Use the Lamb as a model for personal humility in decision-making and relationships.
- **Community Engagement**: Reflect on the New Jerusalem when participating in community-building activities, ensuring inclusivity and compassion.
- **Global Responsibility**: Allow the lessons of the Four Horsemen to guide your response to global issues, advocating for peace, equity, and sustainability.

By engaging with Revelation's symbols, we align ourselves with its profound message of hope and transformation, finding guidance for our spiritual journey and our role in creating a more compassionate world.

PART THREE

BRINGING REVELATION TO LIFE IN A POSITIVE AND PRODUCTIVE WAY

Revelation's teachings are not confined to symbolic imagery or distant prophecy—they are a call to live with purpose, hope, and compassion. By actively incorporating its principles into daily life, we can create a ripple effect of positivity and transformation.

1. Cultivating Personal Growth Through Revelation's Teachings

Personal transformation begins with small, consistent practices rooted in Revelation's themes of renewal, love, and unity.

- **Morning Reflection**: Start your day with a question: How can I embody humility and compassion today, as exemplified by the Lamb? Use this intention to guide your actions.
- **Affirmation Practices**: Write affirmations inspired by Revelation's symbols, such as: *I am a vessel of renewal and love, bringing harmony to my world.*
- **Gratitude Journaling**: End your day by listing ways you witnessed or contributed to renewal, justice, or unity. Reflect on how these moments align with Revelation's vision.

These practices not only deepen spiritual awareness but also foster a positive mindset that aligns with Revelation's call to transformation.

2. Building Meaningful Connections in Communities

Revelation emphasizes collective harmony and the power of united action. Bringing this vision to life means creating inclusive, supportive communities.

- **Host a Study Circle**: Organize a small group to explore Revelation's teachings and discuss practical ways to implement them in your community.
- **Start a Community Project**: Tangible projects, such as a food pantry, a community garden, or an interfaith dialogue, bring Revelation's call for unity to life.
- **Engage in Conflict Resolution**: Inspired by Revelation's emphasis on reconciliation, take active steps to mediate conflicts within your community, fostering understanding and peace.

Through these initiatives, we reflect Revelation's vision of the New Jerusalem, a space where diversity is celebrated, and compassion thrives.

3. Inspiring Global Change Through Revelation's Principles

Revelation's call extends to global stewardship, urging us to care for creation and advocate for justice.

- **Environmental Stewardship**: Join reforestation efforts, clean-up drives, or support sustainable practices that reflect the renewal promised in Revelation's imagery of a restored Earth.
- **Advocate for Justice**: Partner with organizations addressing global inequality, such as supporting refugees, fighting hunger, or promoting education.
- **Participate in Global Dialogues**: Engage in international forums or online platforms that promote peace and understanding, reflecting Revelation's vision of unity among nations.

By acting on these global issues, we extend Revelation's message beyond personal transformation to a collective mission for a better world.

4. Living Revelation's Teachings in Long-Term Commitments

True transformation requires sustained effort and commitment to Revelation's principles.

- **Create a Family Legacy**: Establish traditions, such as annual service projects or reflection gatherings, that pass Revelation's teachings to future generations.
- **Found a Nonprofit or Advocacy Group**: Align your efforts with Revelation's call for renewal by addressing specific social, environmental, or spiritual needs.
- **Mentorship and Education**: Teach others about Revelation's themes of hope and unity, empowering them to apply these lessons in their own lives.

These commitments ensure that Revelation's vision continues to inspire and guide future generations.

PART FOUR

SACRED CONNECTIONS: BUILDING A COLLECTIVE VISION

Revelation's call resonates far beyond individual transformation—it invites us into a grand narrative of collective action and shared purpose. At its core, the text envisions a world where justice, inclusivity, and harmony define human interactions. Revelation challenges us to reimagine relationships, build meaningful connections, and align our lives with divine principles to create a world reflective of the New Jerusalem's vision of peace and unity.

In this chapter, we delve deeply into how Revelation inspires sacred connections through interfaith dialogue, justice advocacy, environmental stewardship, and strengthened community bonds. Each step toward collective renewal embodies Revelation's timeless call for transformation and unity.

Fostering Interfaith Dialogue: Bridging Divides, Building Unity

Revelation's vision of a unified humanity finds expression in its portrayal of the New Jerusalem, where all nations and peoples come together under divine guidance. This vision underscores the importance of fostering interfaith dialogue—a practice that transcends religious and cultural boundaries to build understanding, respect, and solidarity.

Creating Spaces for Shared Understanding

- **Community Events:** Organize interfaith gatherings like panel discussions, cultural festivals, or shared meals that celebrate the common values of compassion, hope, and love. Imagine a community where diverse voices come together to exchange ideas, share traditions, and foster mutual respect.
- **Shared Worship Experiences:** Arrange moments of collective prayer, meditation, or music from different faith traditions. These

shared spiritual practices cultivate a sense of connection and solidarity across belief systems.

Education as a Tool for Unity

- **Workshops and Seminars:** Develop programs that explore the histories, teachings, and practices of various faiths. By dispelling misconceptions and promoting empathy, such initiatives build bridges between communities.
- **Youth Engagement:** Engage young people in interfaith activities, teaching them the importance of respect and collaboration from an early age.

The Impact of Dialogue

Through interfaith dialogue, we create a tapestry of shared humanity, reflecting Revelation's call for unity in diversity. These efforts remind us that while our beliefs may differ, our shared desire for justice, love, and peace connects us.

Advocating for Justice and Equity: A Call to Action

The fall of Babylon in Revelation symbolizes the collapse of oppressive systems and the triumph of righteousness. This powerful imagery inspires us to confront systemic inequities and advocate for marginalized communities, bringing Revelation's message of justice to life.

Local Advocacy: Transforming Communities

- **Empowering the Marginalized:** Create platforms where underrepresented voices can be heard, ensuring their stories shape community priorities. For example, organize storytelling nights or town hall meetings that center the experiences of marginalized groups.
- **Collaboration with Organizations:** Partner with local charities, food banks, and shelters to provide essential resources for underserved populations.

- **Mentorship and Job Training:** Develop programs that equip individuals from disadvantaged backgrounds with skills and opportunities for economic independence.

Driving Systemic Change

- **Policy Advocacy:** Campaign for reforms that address social inequities, such as affordable housing, accessible healthcare, and equitable education. Work with local leaders to influence policies that align with Revelation's vision of justice.
- **Amplifying Activism:** Support global movements addressing inequality, such as fair-trade initiatives or campaigns combating human trafficking.

Justice as Worship

Advocating for justice is not just a social act—it's a spiritual one. Revelation reminds us that aligning with righteousness reflects divine intention and brings us closer to creating a world where compassion and equity reign.

Promoting Environmental Stewardship: Caring for Creation

Revelation's ecological imagery, from the River of Life to the New Heaven and New Earth, highlights the sacredness of creation and humanity's responsibility to nurture it. Environmental stewardship is an act of faith that aligns us with divine harmony and sustains the world for future generations.

Practical Steps for Environmental Care

- **Daily Sustainability:** Adopt small but impactful habits, such as reducing single-use plastics, conserving energy, and composting.
- **Community Clean-Ups:** Organize events to clean parks, rivers, and neighborhoods. These actions foster a shared sense of responsibility for the environment.
- **Reforestation Projects:** Partner with local or global organizations to plant trees, restoring ecosystems and mitigating climate change.

Advocating for Climate Action

- **Policy Engagement:** Support initiatives that promote renewable energy, protect biodiversity, and reduce carbon emissions. Advocate for sustainable city planning and green infrastructure.
- **Education and Awareness:** Host workshops on topics like sustainable farming, water conservation, and the importance of protecting natural habitats.

A Vision of Renewal

By caring for the Earth, we honor Revelation's vision of a restored creation. Each effort to protect and heal the environment reflects our commitment to divine stewardship and the interconnectedness of all life.

Strengthening Community Bonds: Building Sacred Connections

Revelation's vision of the New Jerusalem celebrates collective harmony and collaboration. To bring this vision into reality, we must nurture deeper connections within our own communities.

Practical Ways to Foster Unity

- **Mentorship Programs:** Create initiatives that connect generations, pairing youth with elders to exchange wisdom, skills, and fresh perspectives.
- **Cultural Celebrations:** Host events that honor your community's traditions, cuisines, and stories, fostering mutual respect and pride.
- **Skill-Sharing Networks:** Organize workshops where members can teach and learn from one another, building a culture of mutual support and empowerment.
- **Conflict Resolution Training:** Through workshops that emphasize active listening and empathy, equip communities with tools for effective communication and understanding.

Shared Projects for Collective Growth

- **Community Storytelling Circles:** Invite members to share personal experiences and histories, creating spaces of connection and understanding.
- **Artistic Collaborations:** Work together on projects like murals or community gardens that embody shared values and goals.
- **Neighborhood Support Networks:** Develop systems to check on vulnerable individuals, ensuring no one feels isolated or forgotten.

Celebrating Together

Revelation often describes moments of worship and joy. Communities can mirror this by creating events focused on gratitude, renewal, and shared purpose. Whether through interfaith dialogues, holiday celebrations, or music festivals, these gatherings strengthen bonds and inspire collective hope.

A Vision for Collective Renewal: Living Revelation's Call

Revelation is not just a book to be studied—it is a call to action, a guide for building a world rooted in love, justice, and harmony. By fostering interfaith dialogue, advocating for justice, caring for creation, and strengthening community bonds, we bring its teachings to life.

Each connection we forge, and every action we take contributes to the collective vision of a world aligned with divine purpose. Through collaboration and compassion, we can transform Revelation's vision of the New Jerusalem into a living reality—one where inclusivity, renewal, and peace define our shared existence.

Let Revelation inspire you to take bold steps toward building sacred connections. Together, we can create a legacy of love and unity that reflects its eternal truths, shaping a future filled with hope and purpose.

PART FIVE

BUILDING LASTING LEGACIES OF FAITH AND ACTION

Revelation's call is timeless, challenging us to live in ways that reflect its vision of renewal, justice, and unity. It pushes us to think beyond personal transformation, urging us to create legacies that endure—a tapestry woven with acts of faith, compassion, and systemic advocacy. Such legacies ensure that Revelation's teachings are not just historical or symbolic but living principles that shape the world for generations to come.

This chapter explores how to craft meaningful legacy projects, advocate for systemic change, and inspire collective transformation through tangible actions rooted in Revelation's eternal truths.

Establishing a Legacy Project: Aligning Faith with Enduring Impact

A legacy project is a bridge between personal values and meaningful actions, offering the chance to leave a lasting mark that embodies Revelation's principles of justice, inclusivity, and hope.

Community Initiatives: Planting Seeds of Unity and Growth

Creating local projects is a tangible way to foster change and build connections within your community.

- **Community Gardens:** These green spaces symbolize growth, renewal, and collaboration. Involve schools, senior centers, and local organizations to cultivate not only food but also a sense of belonging and shared purpose.
- **Educational Programs:** Literacy initiatives or after-school tutoring programs empower the next generation, breaking cycles of poverty and ignorance while embodying Revelation's call for equity and enlightenment.

Spiritual Traditions: Inspiring Through Shared Practices

Establish traditions that invite reflection, unity, and service.

- **Annual Days of Service:** Inspired by Revelation's themes, organize yearly events where diverse groups come together for acts of kindness, like distributing care packages, cleaning public spaces, or hosting interfaith discussions.
- **Seasonal Celebrations:** Create recurring events that align with Revelation's imagery, such as planting trees during spring to honor renewal or lighting candles during winter as a symbol of hope.

Philanthropic Efforts: Supporting Long-Term Change

Philanthropy allows individuals to channel resources into causes aligned with Revelation's teachings.

- **Scholarship Funds:** Establish scholarships for underprivileged youth, giving them access to education and opportunities that align with Revelation's vision of equity.
- **Targeted Donations:** Partner with nonprofits that focus on justice, environmental care, or community empowerment. For instance, funding clean water initiatives or supporting refugee assistance programs mirrors Revelation's emphasis on restoration.

Creative Contributions: Immortalizing Revelation's Message

Art, music, and literature can be powerful tools for spreading Revelation's principles.

- **Public Art Projects:** Murals depicting Revelation's symbols, such as the Tree of Life or the River of Life, can inspire reflection and dialogue within communities.
- **Thematic Workshops:** Host writing or music workshops focused on themes of renewal and justice, encouraging participants to explore their own spiritual journeys through creativity.

By embedding Revelation's values into these projects, we create touchstones of hope and inspiration for future generations.

Advocating for Systemic Change: Transforming Society with Revelation's Vision

Revelation not only calls for individual renewal but also challenges us to confront and reshape the systems that perpetuate inequality, corruption, and harm. Advocacy is essential to align societal structures with divine principles of justice and harmony.

Social Justice Movements: Confronting Inequity

The fall of Babylon in Revelation symbolizes the collapse of oppressive systems. Today, this imagery inspires efforts to dismantle racism, sexism, and economic disparity.

- **Volunteer Engagement:** Join organizations that address systemic inequities, whether through mentoring programs for underserved youth or providing legal aid for marginalized groups.
- **Peaceful Activism:** Participate in protests and campaigns that demand justice, ensuring that your actions are rooted in nonviolence and compassion.

Environmental Action: Caring for Creation

Revelation's vision of a New Heaven and New Earth emphasizes the sacredness of creation and humanity's role in its stewardship.

- **Sustainability Efforts:** Reduce personal waste, support local recycling initiatives, and advocate for policies that promote renewable energy.
- **Reforestation and Conservation:** Engage in tree-planting drives, habitat restoration projects, and efforts to protect endangered species, reflecting Revelation's ecological themes.

Policy Engagement: Driving Systemic Change

Effective advocacy often requires influencing policies that shape society's future.

- **Education Reform:** Campaign for equitable access to quality education, ensuring that all children have opportunities to learn and grow.
- **Healthcare Access:** Advocate for affordable healthcare as a fundamental human right, aligning with Revelation's call for inclusivity and care.
- **Environmental Legislation:** Support laws that address climate change and promote sustainable development, ensuring a better world for future generations.

Empowering Marginalized Voices: Elevating the Silenced

Revelation's vision of inclusivity compels us to amplify the voices of those often ignored.

- **Platform Creation:** Develop forums where marginalized individuals can share their stories, helping to shape community and policy decisions.
- **Mentorship Programs:** Pair mentors with individuals from underrepresented groups to provide guidance and open pathways for advancement.

By advocating for systemic change, we turn Revelation's prophetic vision into actionable goals that uplift humanity and reflect divine justice.

Combining Legacy and Advocacy: Transformative Impact

The power of combining personal legacy projects with systemic advocacy lies in its ability to inspire both immediate and lasting change. These efforts ripple outward, influencing not only individual lives but also societal structures.

Inspiring Collective Transformation

- **Ripple Effects of Advocacy:** One scholarship can uplift a family; one community garden can strengthen neighborhoods. When these efforts are combined with systemic change, the impact grows exponentially.

- **Generational Influence:** Legacy projects inspire younger generations to take up the mantle of justice and renewal, creating a culture of continuous transformation.

Building Communities of Hope

- **Interconnected Actions:** Align personal projects with broader movements to create a cohesive vision of renewal. For example, a literacy program might collaborate with education reform campaigns, amplifying their reach and impact.
- **Shared Goals:** Foster a sense of shared purpose within communities, reminding members that their collective actions contribute to a divine vision of harmony.

The Enduring Power of Legacy

Revelation's teachings remind us that we are not merely individuals navigating isolated paths but participants in a greater divine story. By crafting lasting legacies and advocating for systemic change, we align our lives with its call for justice, compassion, and renewal.

Imagine the impact of these efforts: communities transformed by gardens that feed both body and soul, children empowered by education and opportunity, and systems reshaped to reflect equity and fairness. Each action, rooted in faith and guided by Revelation's vision, becomes a testament to divine love and hope.

Practical Steps to Build Your Legacy

1. Identify a cause or need that aligns with your values and Revelation's teachings.
2. Plan a project or advocacy effort that addresses this need, ensuring it reflects principles of justice, inclusivity, and renewal.
3. Collaborate with others to amplify your efforts and build lasting impact.

A Call to Action: Creating a World That Reflects Revelation

Revelation is not just a text to study—it is a call to live boldly, to act with purpose, and to build a legacy that reflects divine principles. Whether through personal projects or systemic advocacy, each step we take brings us closer to its vision of unity, justice, and harmony.

Let Revelation inspire you to craft a legacy of faith and action, ensuring its teachings resonate for generations to come. Together, we can transform its vision into reality, creating a world rooted in love, compassion, and divine renewal.

PART SIX

REVELATION'S CONNECTION TO THE REST OF SCRIPTURE

The Book of Revelation is far more than a dramatic conclusion to the Bible—it is a profound culmination of divine themes that weave throughout Scripture, uniting the past, present, and future into a cohesive narrative. Every symbol, prophecy, and vision in Revelation finds its roots in earlier biblical texts, highlighting its interconnectedness with the rest of Scripture. Through these connections, Revelation reveals itself as not just an apocalyptic vision but as a guide to understanding God's eternal plan for creation, humanity, and ultimate renewal.

This chapter explores the rich tapestry of Revelation's connections with other biblical texts, uncovering deeper meanings that illuminate its role in the grand story of divine truth and human transformation.

1. Revelation as the Culmination of Biblical Themes

Revelation serves as the final chapter of the Bible's grand narrative, bringing to fulfillment the promises, prophecies, and symbols introduced throughout Scripture. It completes the story, offering a vision of restoration and divine triumph that echoes the foundational themes of earlier texts.

Genesis to Revelation: Creation to New Creation

The Bible begins with Genesis, the story of creation, and concludes with Revelation's vision of the New Creation. These bookends frame the entire biblical narrative, highlighting God's unwavering commitment to renewal.

The Tree of Life:

The Tree of Life, first introduced in Genesis, reappears in Revelation 22, standing at the center of the New Jerusalem. In

Genesis, humanity's access to the tree is lost through sin; in Revelation, it is restored, symbolizing eternal life and harmony with God.

- **Why This Matters:** This continuity underscores God's unchanging nature and plan. What was lost in Eden is redeemed in Revelation, assuring us that divine restoration is always within reach.

The Garden and the City:

Genesis begins with a garden, a place of intimacy with God, while Revelation ends with a city, a symbol of perfected community. This progression reflects the journey from individual connection to collective renewal, showing that God's plan encompasses both personal and societal transformation.

Prophecies Fulfilled in Revelation

Revelation's imagery often mirrors the prophecies of Isaiah, Ezekiel, Daniel, and other Old Testament texts, reinforcing its role as the culmination of biblical prophecy.

Isaiah's Vision of a New Heaven and New Earth (Isaiah 65:17): Isaiah foretells a world free from pain and sorrow, a vision that aligns with Revelation 21's depiction of the New Jerusalem.

Daniel's Beasts and Revelation's Beast:

Daniel's visions of beasts representing oppressive empires find their counterpart in Revelation's depiction of the Beast, symbolizing the ultimate triumph of God over evil powers.

- **Why This Matters:** These connections deepen our appreciation of Revelation as a fulfillment of divine prophecy, linking the Old and New Testaments in a unified story of hope and justice.

2. Revelation's Message of Hope Through Judgment

Judgment is a central theme in Revelation, often depicted through vivid imagery of plagues, cosmic upheavals, and divine wrath.

While these scenes can evoke fear, their ultimate purpose is to awaken humanity to the consequences of straying from God's principles and to highlight the promise of redemption.

Why Fear Exists

Revelation's intense imagery, from the Four Horsemen to the Seven Bowls of Wrath, often stirs feelings of dread. However, fear is not the goal—it is a catalyst for reflection and transformation.

- Isaiah's Call to Repentance:

Like Revelation, Isaiah uses stark imagery to call for repentance, urging humanity to return to God's ways. Both texts emphasize that judgment serves as a pathway to renewal rather than an endpoint of despair.

Hope Paired with Judgment

Revelation consistently balances its depictions of judgment with promises of redemption. For example:

- **The Seven Bowls of Wrath (Revelation 16):** These plagues are immediately followed by the vision of the New Jerusalem, a city of peace and renewal.
- **Why This Matters:** Judgment is not punitive but transformative, serving as a necessary step toward enlightenment and restoration.

3. Revelation's Role in Divine Storytelling

Revelation is the Bible's grand finale, tying together the threads of God's story while providing resolution to its conflicts and promises.

The Lamb as Fulfillment of the Sacrificial Lamb

The Lamb in Revelation, depicted as both slain and triumphant, fulfills the symbolism of the sacrificial lamb in Exodus, which marked Israel's deliverance from Egypt.

- **Why This Matters:** The Lamb embodies divine love and victory through sacrifice, linking the story of liberation in Exodus to the ultimate deliverance promised in Revelation.

Interconnected Symbols Across Scripture

- **The Bride of Christ:**
  Introduced in the Gospels and Epistles, the Bride of Christ represents the Church, prepared and perfected for union with Christ. This theme reaches its fulfillment in Revelation's New Jerusalem, described as a bride adorned for her husband.
- **The Scroll and the Word:**
  The sealed scroll in Revelation mirrors the scrolls of prophecy in Ezekiel and Isaiah, emphasizing the continuity of God's revelation and the unfolding of His divine plan.

4. Revelation's Call for Reflection

Revelation is not just a narrative—it is an invitation to reflect on our lives and align with divine principles.

Personal Reflection

Revelation's vivid imagery challenges readers to examine their actions, priorities, and spiritual journeys.

- **Questions to Ponder:**
  - How do my choices reflect the values of the New Jerusalem—justice, unity, and compassion?
  - What trials in my life mirror Revelation's tribulations, and how can I face them with faith and perseverance?

Collective Reflection

Revelation also calls on communities to embody its vision of renewal.

- **Practical Applications:**
  - Foster inclusivity and justice within your community, reflecting the harmony of the New Heaven and New Earth.
  - Collaborate on initiatives that promote reconciliation and healing, echoing Revelation's promise of restoration.

5. Revelation's Connection to the Life of Christ

Revelation's themes are deeply intertwined with Jesus Christ's teachings and ministry, providing a bridge between the Gospels and the New Testament's eschatological vision.

Jesus as the Alpha and Omega

Revelation repeatedly refers to Jesus as the Alpha and Omega, the beginning and the end. This title encapsulates Christ's role as the foundation and fulfillment of God's plan.

- **Why This Matters:** It reminds us that Christ's teachings in the Gospels are the key to understanding Revelation's visions, emphasizing love, sacrifice, and hope.

The Kingdom of God:

Revelation's New Jerusalem represents the fulfillment of Jesus' teachings about the Kingdom of God—a realm of justice, peace, and divine presence.

Conclusion: Revelation's Unified Message

Revelation is the capstone of Scripture, uniting the Bible's overarching themes into a single, profound vision of hope and renewal. From Genesis to Revelation, the narrative of creation, fall, redemption, and restoration unfolds, revealing God's unwavering commitment to humanity and His ultimate plan for renewal.

By connecting Revelation with other scriptures, we uncover its role as a guide—not to instill fear but to inspire action, transformation, and faith. Its vivid imagery and interconnected symbols challenge us to reflect deeply, live intentionally, and contribute to God's eternal story of love and restoration.

As the final book of the Bible, Revelation reminds us that every ending is a new beginning, urging us to embrace its message with purpose and hope. In its pages, we find not only the culmination of divine truth but also the promise of a world renewed—a vision that calls us to live with faith, compassion, and a steadfast commitment to God's plan.

PART SEVEN

REVELATION'S ETERNAL JOURNEY – PERSONAL AND COLLECTIVE TRANSFORMATION

Revelation is more than a vision of the end times; it is a living guide that calls us to align with divine purpose through personal growth and collective unity. Its teachings weave through the fabric of life, inviting individuals and communities to embody faith, hope, and renewal. The eternal journey described in Revelation is not a static destination but an ever-unfolding process of transformation, one that bridges the internal and external, the personal and the global.

In this chapter, we explore how Revelation inspires profound changes within the soul, fosters unity across humanity, and offers practical pathways for creating enduring legacies rooted in its teachings.

1. The Soul's Eternal Journey: Embracing Personal Transformation

Revelation invites each individual to embark on a spiritual pilgrimage, using its rich symbolism and themes as guides for personal growth. This inward journey is marked by moments of challenge, renewal, and awakening.

Understanding the Symbols as Personal Guides

Revelation's imagery is more than apocalyptic drama; it serves as a mirror for the soul's inner struggles and triumphs.

- **The Lamb as a Model for Life:** Representing humility, love, and sacrifice, the Lamb urges us to approach life's challenges with compassion and grace. It reminds us that true strength lies in vulnerability and service.
- **The Seven Seals and Inner Awakening:** The seals can be seen as stages of spiritual growth—beginning with confronting fears

and culminating in the peace that comes from trust in divine guidance.

Daily Practices for Spiritual Growth

- **Morning Reflections:** Begin each day by meditating on Revelation's imagery, such as the New Jerusalem or the River of Life. Let these symbols inspire acts of kindness, inclusion, and mindfulness throughout your day.
- **Journaling for Renewal:** Record personal challenges and victories, drawing parallels to Revelation's themes of struggle and triumph. Reflect on how faith has helped you overcome obstacles and embrace change.

Cycles of Renewal: Embracing Change

Revelation's depiction of destruction leading to renewal mirrors the cycles of transformation in our lives.

- **Insight:** Just as Revelation shows the old passing away to make room for the new, personal growth often requires letting go of outdated habits, relationships, or beliefs.
- **Practical Application:** Identify areas in your life that need renewal and take intentional steps to embrace change as part of your spiritual journey.

2. Collective Enlightenment: Building a Unified Humanity

Revelation's vision of the New Jerusalem calls not only for personal transformation but also for collective action. It is an invitation to work together in building a world rooted in justice, equity, and compassion.

Applying the Vision of the New Jerusalem

The New Jerusalem, where all nations and peoples gather in harmony, offers a blueprint for creating inclusive and unified communities.

- **Collaboration Across Differences:** Organize interfaith service projects, cultural exchanges, or community dialogues to foster understanding and cooperation among diverse groups.
- **Advocating for Justice:** Support policies and initiatives that promote fairness and compassion, such as affordable housing, healthcare access, and education reform. These actions embody Revelation's call for equity and unity.

Creating Sustainable Communities

Environmental stewardship and community resilience are vital to reflecting Revelation's vision of renewal.

- **Urban Gardening and Renewable Energy:** Establish practices that care for the Earth, such as urban gardens that feed both body and spirit or renewable energy projects that reduce ecological impact.
- **Conflict Resolution and Healing:** Address local tensions by organizing events that promote reconciliation and understanding, such as peacebuilding workshops or restorative justice circles.

Engaging Globally for Change

Revelation's call extends beyond local communities to encompass the entire world.

- **Supporting Global Causes:** Participate in efforts to combat climate change, alleviate poverty, and promote human rights.
- **Building International Connections:** Collaborate with organizations that foster global solidarity, emphasizing shared values of justice and renewal.

3. Practical Legacy Creation: Ensuring Revelation's Teachings Endure

To ensure Revelation's timeless message resonates through generations, we are called to create lasting legacies rooted in its principles of renewal, justice, and love.

Family and Community Traditions

- **Annual Reflections:** Establish shared practices such as yearly family discussions or community events centered on Revelation's themes. For example, dedicate a day to acts of service inspired by its call for compassion and equity.
- **Generational Storytelling:** Pass down stories of personal and communal triumphs that reflect Revelation's values, connecting younger generations to its teachings.

Creative Expressions of Faith

- **Artistic Reinterpretation:** Use art, music, or literature to bring Revelation's symbols to life in ways that resonate with modern audiences. For example, compose music inspired by the River of Life or paint murals of the New Jerusalem.
- **Workshops and Exhibits:** Organize events that connect Revelation's teachings to contemporary challenges, such as addressing climate change or fostering social justice.

Mentorship and Education

- **Guiding the Next Generation:** Mentor others in applying Revelation's principles to their lives. This could take the form of faith-based study groups or personal mentorship focused on integrating spiritual growth with social impact.
- **Creating Opportunities:** Establish scholarships or educational programs that emphasize Revelation's values of equity, renewal, and justice.

4. Bridging Personal and Collective Transformation

Revelation emphasizes the interconnectedness of personal growth and collective action. By nurturing the soul, we strengthen our capacity to contribute to a more just and unified world.

Balancing Inner and Outer Work

- **Inner Reflection:** Use Revelation's teachings as a guide for self-improvement, examining how personal habits and attitudes align with its vision of renewal.
- **Outer Service:** Extend these lessons outward by participating in community initiatives, such as volunteering, mentoring, or advocacy.

Finding Strength in Unity

Revelation's vision of diverse peoples united in harmony reminds us that individual transformation contributes to a greater collective story.

- **Building Partnerships:** Collaborate with others who share your values to amplify efforts toward justice, equity, and renewal.

Celebrating Progress

Revelation's message of triumph encourages us to mark milestones in our journey, both individually and collectively.

- **Personal Milestones:** Celebrate moments of spiritual growth, such as overcoming a fear or fostering a new habit.
- **Community Achievements:** Honor collective progress, such as completing a community project or resolving local conflicts, as reflections of Revelation's promise of harmony.

5. Revelation as a Living Journey

Revelation is not a static prophecy but a dynamic guide, calling us to participate in an ongoing process of renewal and alignment with divine purpose. It challenges us to see life as a journey where each step—whether personal growth or collective action—brings us closer to the eternal vision of love and restoration.

Living with Intention

- **Daily Alignment:** Begin each day with a moment of reflection on Revelation's teachings, asking how you can bring its principles of hope, justice, and renewal into your actions.
- **Faith in Action:** Let Revelation's imagery inspire concrete steps, such as helping a neighbor, advocating for justice, or creating art that uplifts others.

Trusting in Restoration

Revelation assures us that renewal is always possible, even in the face of destruction or despair. This promise invites us to trust in divine love and to act with courage and compassion in every aspect of life.

A Final Reflection: Becoming Co-Creators in the Eternal Journey

Imagine yourself walking through the gates of the New Jerusalem, its light illuminating the path ahead. Each step represents a moment of personal growth, an act of service, or a gesture of kindness. This is Revelation's invitation—to become co-creators in its vision of renewal.

By embracing personal transformation and contributing to collective unity, we fulfill Revelation's call to live with faith, intention, and purpose. Let its teachings guide you to build a world grounded in love, justice, and hope—one step at a time, one soul at a time.

PART EIGHT

THE ETERNAL PROMISE – LIVING AS STEWARDS OF DIVINE UNITY

Introduction: Embracing the Eternal Promise

Revelation is not an ending—it is a timeless call to action. Its teachings invite us to live as stewards of divine unity, embodying its principles through personal transformation, communal engagement, and global responsibility. **Part Eight** explores how we can integrate these sacred lessons into every aspect of life, ensuring they endure as a legacy of hope and renewal for future generations.
Stewardship of Self

The journey begins within. By nurturing our spiritual growth, we align with Revelation's call for renewal and harmony. Cultivating a mindful, intentional approach to life helps us integrate its wisdom into daily practices:

Mindfulness and Meditation: Dedicate time each day to focus on Revelation's symbols. For example:

- Visualize the Lamb as a symbol of humility and reflect on how you can embody this quality in your relationships.
- Meditate on the New Jerusalem's unity to foster inner peace and harmony.

Journaling for Insight: Each evening, reflect on moments when your actions aligned with Revelation's teachings—acts of kindness, patience, or forgiveness. Write them down to deepen self-awareness and reinforce these values.

Intentional Living: Start each morning with an intention inspired by Revelation's themes, such as promoting peace or practicing gratitude. Carry this focus into your actions and interactions throughout the day.

Commitment to Growth: Set weekly goals that reflect Revelation's principles. For instance:

- Choose to forgive someone who has wronged you.
- Practice patience in challenging situations.
- Volunteer in your community to embody selflessness.

By stewarding our hearts and minds, we create a foundation for living Revelation's promise with purpose and authenticity.

Stewardship of Community

Revelation's vision of unity calls us to build compassionate and just communities. By fostering connections and addressing communal challenges, we reflect its teachings in our collective lives:

Inclusive Practices:

- Organize events in your neighborhood or workplace that celebrate diversity, such as cultural festivals or interfaith dialogues.
- Start a book club centered on spiritual or thought-provoking themes to create a safe space for meaningful discussions.

Service Initiatives:

- Participate in or organize projects such as food drives, mentoring programs, or neighborhood clean-ups.
- Collaborate with others to plant a community garden, symbolizing renewal and shared growth.

Conflict Resolution:

- Use Revelation's message of renewal as a guide to mediate and resolve disputes in your community.
- Create support groups or workshops to teach effective communication and empathy, fostering understanding and peace.

Strong communities rooted in love, inclusivity, and service embody the unity and renewal at the heart of Revelation's vision.

Stewardship of the World

Revelation's promise extends beyond the self and community to encompass the care of creation and the pursuit of global unity. Its teachings inspire us to confront global challenges with faith and resolve:

Environmental Advocacy:

- Join initiatives like reforestation projects or local clean-up drives to honor the Earth as a reflection of Revelation's renewed creation.
- Advocate for sustainable practices in your community, such as reducing waste, conserving energy, or supporting renewable energy solutions.

Interfaith Cooperation:

- Engage with organizations like Religions for Peace or the United Religions Initiative, which promote collaboration across faiths to address global issues like poverty and conflict.

Humanitarian Efforts:

- Support causes that care for the vulnerable, such as disaster relief, refugee assistance, or providing clean water to underserved communities.
- Contribute to organizations like the Red Cross, UNHCR, or Charity: Water to mirror Revelation's call for justice and compassion.

By addressing these global challenges, we bring Revelation's principles of renewal, justice, and unity into tangible actions, contributing to a more harmonious and compassionate world.

Practical Actions: Living the Promise

To make Revelation's teachings tangible and impactful, integrate these practices into your routine:

Daily:

- Begin each morning with a meditation on a symbol from Revelation, such as the Lamb or the New Jerusalem.
- Let this reflection inspire intentional acts of kindness, gratitude, or humility throughout your day.

Weekly:

- Dedicate time to volunteer or participate in a service project that aligns with Revelation's principles of renewal and justice.

Long-Term:

- Develop a legacy project inspired by Revelation's call for compassion and hope, such as:
- Establishing a scholarship fund.
- Creating a family tradition of giving back during holidays.
- Supporting a charitable initiative that reflects your values and Revelation's vision.

A Final Blessing: Walking with Revelation's Light

As stewards of Revelation's eternal promise, we are called to live with purpose and grace. Reflect on its teachings and let them illuminate your path:

Quiet Reflection: Meditate in a peaceful space, visualizing yourself as a vessel of divine unity. Imagine carrying this light into all areas of your life.

Personal Mission: Write down one action you will take this week to embody Revelation's principles, such as practicing forgiveness, extending kindness, or serving others.

Gratitude Prayer: Offer a prayer of thanks for Revelation's wisdom, asking for guidance in aligning your actions with its eternal promise.

Blessing

May the wisdom of Revelation illuminate your path, The courage of its teachings strengthens your resolve, And the unity of its vision guides you to create a world reflecting divine love and renewal.

Go forth as stewards of hope, carrying its light into every corner of your life. Let Revelation's eternal promise inspire your actions, shape your relationships, and guide your vision for the future.

PART NINE

NEW INSIGHTS INTO THE BOOK OF REVELATION

Revelation has long fascinated and mystified readers, its vivid symbols and profound teachings offering a glimpse into divine mysteries. Yet, beneath its enigmatic surface lies a timeless guide for understanding the human spirit, the divine purpose, and the bonds that unite creation. **Part Nine** invites readers to step into the story of Revelation anew, uncovering its relevance for modern life and discovering its power to transform how we see ourselves and the world.

Revelation as a Blueprint for Spiritual Growth

Imagine Revelation not as a distant prophecy, but as a personal invitation to grow. Each word, each image, feels alive, guiding us toward understanding our place in the divine plan.

The story begins with the Seven Churches, each representing a universal struggle:

- The Church of Ephesus calls us back to lost passion.
- Smyrna urges us to face fear with faith.
- Sardis warns against the lull of complacency.

These churches speak to us all, reflecting the spiritual hurdles we encounter and calling us to examine our own hearts. Revelation doesn't unfold in a straight line but mirrors life's cyclical nature—the ending of one chapter always leads to the beginning of another. Death gives way to renewal. Struggle precedes transformation. It's in this rhythm that Revelation teaches its most profound lesson: **hope beyond hardship**.

Think of the seals, trumpets, and bowls not as omens of despair, but as metaphors for the trials we all face. They remind us that every storm carries the promise of a new dawn. In the face of life's greatest challenges, Revelation whispers, "This is not the end. Renewal awaits."

The Language of Symbols: A Mirror to Inner and Outer Realities

Revelation speaks through symbols, each one a vivid brushstroke painting of the realities we live within and without.

The **Beast** and the **Dragon** roar across its pages, not as distant terrors, but as echoes of the chaos within us:

In moments of fear, insecurity, or anger, their shadows flicker in our hearts.

On a societal level, they represent division and systemic injustice, challenging us to stand against oppression and inequality.

In contrast, the **New Jerusalem** shines as a beacon of hope. Beyond its golden streets and jeweled walls lies a deeper meaning—a vision of spiritual unity and peace. It calls us to strive for harmony: in our relationships, in our communities, and in our care for the Earth.

Then there are the **White Robes of the Martyrs**, their brilliance a testament to steadfast faith. They remind us that even in the face of injustice, courage and integrity prevail. These symbols aren't just relics of ancient visions; they're guides, calling us to reflect on the battles within ourselves and the steps we take to create a just world.

A Call to Collective Responsibility

As the narrative of Revelation unfolds, it becomes clear: this isn't a solitary journey. We are part of a greater whole, woven into the fabric of humanity and creation itself. Revelation's vision of renewal extends beyond personal transformation—it's a charge to unite in purpose.

- **Creating Sacred Spaces:** Whether it's planting a peace garden, building an interfaith center, or simply fostering harmony in your home, these spaces reflect divine unity.

- **Global Stewardship:** Revelation's call to "renew the Earth" urges us to act. From addressing climate change to protecting endangered species, our care for creation echoes its promise of restoration.
- **Confronting Inequality:** Revelation challenges us to build a just world. By advocating for education, healthcare, and economic fairness, we answer its call to stand against inequity.

Together, these acts of stewardship remind us of our shared responsibility to carry the light of Revelation into the world.

Revelation's Relevance to Modern Challenges

Though centuries old, Revelation speaks with startling clarity to the complexities of today's world. Its battles are not confined to apocalyptic visions—they mirror the conflicts we navigate in our daily lives.

The **Lamb's Message of Peace** offers a path forward:

- In times of division, it calls us to reconciliation.
- In an era of technological overreach, it urges us to use innovation to connect rather than divide.
- In moments of doubt, it empowers us to see ourselves as co-creators of harmony.

Revelation's vivid imagery isn't meant to provoke fear but to inspire awe and remind us of our purpose. Each symbol, each passage, becomes a compass, guiding us toward resilience, faith, and action. It assures us that love—not destruction—has the final word.

A Timeless Message for a Changing World

As the pace of change accelerates, Revelation's message grows ever more urgent. It invites us to pause amid the noise, finding stillness and clarity in its wisdom.

Consider the silence of the **Seventh Seal**:

- In this moment of quiet, heaven holds its breath, inviting us to do the same.
- This pause reminds us to discern what truly matters and to align our actions with divine purpose.

Revelation also challenges us to reimagine its symbols for our time:

- The **Four Horsemen** become metaphors for modern crises—climate change, economic disparity, conflict, and technological misuse.
- The **New Jerusalem** transforms into a vision of sustainability, equity, and global unity.

Each of us is called to carry Revelation's promise into this new era. By fostering innovation, addressing injustices, and building bridges across divides, we participate in the eternal story of renewal.

Rediscovering Revelation's Promise

Even as the world around us shifts, Revelation's core truth remains constant: transformation is the pathway to renewal. It teaches us to embrace change with faith, knowing that challenges can lead to deeper alignment with our purpose.

Whether through small daily reflections or grand acts of service, Revelation invites us to become active participants in shaping a future rooted in love, justice, and unity. As its timeless narrative unfolds, it offers reassurance that even amid uncertainty, the promise of renewal endures.

Closing Reflection

Picture yourself as part of Revelation's story, its symbols coming alive in your life. The Lamb's humility becomes your own. The New Jerusalem's harmony shapes your actions. And the silence of the Seventh Seal offers you the space to reflect and grow.

Revelation is not an ancient riddle to solve—it's a living promise. One that calls each of us to walk with hope, act with purpose, and trust in the divine harmony that holds all things together.

PART TEN

A JOURNEY INTO THE DEPTHS OF REVELATION – INSIGHTS FOR A MODERN AGE

Revelation unfolds like a celestial tapestry, its vivid imagery both beautiful and bewildering. It's not a simple tale but an intricate mosaic of divine truths, its secrets waiting to be unraveled. As you delve deeper into its mysteries, you find that Revelation is more than prophecy—it's an invitation. It invites you to reflect, to act, and to live with purpose, bridging the ancient with the now, the mystical with the practical.

The Cosmic Vision: A Glimpse into Eternity

Imagine yourself standing in Revelation's throne room, a realm where the heavens open to reveal the grandeur of divine unity. Around the central throne are twenty-four elders, their crowns glinting like starlight, and four living creatures that seem to pulse with life itself. They sing, "Holy, holy, holy," a hymn that echoes through eternity.

This isn't just a vision for John; it's a reminder for us all. The throne room reflects the interconnectedness of everything—heaven and earth, spirit and matter. It calls us to recognize our place in the vast, divine dance of creation.

- **Reflection:** When was the last time you truly felt connected to the world around you? Stand under the night sky, let the stars remind you of your smallness, and yet, your profound belonging. Revelation asks you to feel that connection—not just with the universe, but with the divine pulse that sustains it.

As the story progresses, we encounter the **New**

Heaven and New Earth. The imagery is breathtaking: a world renewed, where sorrow is erased, and harmony reigns. But this isn't merely a vision of a distant future; it's an invitation to participate in renewal now.

- **Action:** How can you be a steward of this promise? Perhaps by planting a tree, caring for your community, or making choices that reflect a love for creation. Each small act becomes a thread in the tapestry of the New Heaven and New Earth.

Angels as Messengers and Guardians

Angels weave through Revelation like threads of gold, their presence is both awe-inspiring and deeply intimate. They blow trumpets, pour bowls, and carry messages from the divine.

One such angel appears with a **little scroll** in Chapter 10, offering it to John to eat. Its taste is sweet, but it turns bitter in his stomach—a profound metaphor for truth. Truth often arrives as a blessing, yet it demands transformation, which can be as challenging as it is beautiful.

- **Reflection:** Think of a time when you faced a truth that altered your path. Perhaps it was bitter at first, yet it brought clarity and growth. Revelation reminds us to embrace these moments, trusting that every transformation leads us closer to the divine.

The Power of Testimony: Bearing Witness

Revelation's story is filled with voices—those who bear witness to truth even in the face of great adversity. The **Two Witnesses** stand as symbols of resilience, their testimony unshaken despite opposition. Their courage calls us to consider our own voice.

And then, beneath the altar, we hear the cry of the **Martyrs**, voices lifted in a plea for justice. These cries resonate with anyone who has ever suffered, anyone who has longed for the world to be made right.

- **Action:** Share your story. Your struggles and triumphs are not just personal—they're threads in the larger story of hope and justice. Whether through writing, speaking, or simple conversations, your testimony can inspire others to find courage and faith.

The Mystery of Divine Timing

Revelation moves with a rhythm all its own, often slowing to moments of profound stillness. Consider the silence that follows the opening of the **Seventh Seal**—a pause so deep that heaven itself seems to listen.

This stillness teaches us the value of waiting, of trusting that the divine plan unfolds not in haste but in perfect time.

- **Reflection:** In your own life, where are you being called to wait? Instead of rushing to the next thing, sit with the quiet. Trust that even in the silence, something sacred is taking shape.

The story of the **Millennium**—a thousand years of peace—invites a similar reflection. It's not about quick fixes but about a long-term commitment to building a world aligned with divine purpose.

- **Action:** What can you nurture today that will bear fruit tomorrow? Whether it's a relationship, a community effort, or a personal goal, Revelation reminds us that lasting peace comes from steady, faithful effort.

Courage in the Face of Fear

Revelation's imagery can feel overwhelming—beasts and plagues, fire and thunder. But beneath these dramatic symbols lies a quiet refrain: **Do not be afraid.**

The Lamb, central to Revelation's narrative, is a symbol of humility and victory. It conquers not with force but with love. It reminds us that true courage isn't the absence of fear but the choice to act in spite of it.

- **Reflection:** What fears hold you back? Picture the Lamb walking beside you, whispering that you are not alone. Step forward with faith, knowing that every act of courage moves you closer to the life you're meant to live.

The Tree of Life: Healing and Renewal

At Revelation's conclusion stands the **Tree of Life**, its branches stretching toward eternity, its leaves meant for the healing of nations. This image is more than a promise; it's a call to action.

Imagine planting seeds—not just in the soil, but in your relationships, your community, and your own heart. Every act of kindness, every step toward justice, becomes part of this great tree, bringing healing to the world.

- **Action:** What seeds can you plant today? Perhaps it's volunteering, forgiving someone, or simply offering a kind word. Revelation reminds us that even the smallest acts can grow into something eternal.

Reframing Fear: Revelation's Deeper Message

The beasts, the plagues, the apocalyptic visions—they're not meant to paralyze us with fear. Instead, they're mirrors, reflecting the battles we face within and around us.

When you look at the **Four Horsemen**, don't see destruction—see the challenges of life: conflict, scarcity, fear. Revelation invites you to confront these challenges with faith, knowing that they are part of the journey to renewal.

And when you hear the cries of judgment, don't hear condemnation—hear a call to reflection, a chance to realign with divine purpose.

- **Reflection:** How can you reframe the struggles in your life? Instead of seeing them as obstacles, view them as opportunities for growth. Revelation teaches us that every trial carries the seed of transformation.

A Closing Reflection

Revelation isn't a puzzle to solve or a code to crack—it's a story to live. It's a reminder that we are part of something vast and sacred, that our choices matter, and that renewal is always within reach.

Imagine yourself standing at the gates of the **New Jerusalem**, its light spilling onto your path. The Tree of Life stretches before you, its branches beckoning. This is your story—a story of hope, courage, and transformation.

Step into it. Let its wisdom guide you. And let its light shape the way you live, love, and dream.

PART ELEVEN

REDISCOVERING REVELATION – CLEARING THE MIST

Revelation is often shrouded in misunderstanding, its vivid imagery and dramatic tone sparking fear, confusion, and even dismissal. But imagine stepping into its pages—not as a cryptic puzzle or a terrifying prophecy—but as a vast, symbolic tapestry. What if Revelation is not about predicting doom but about unveiling profound spiritual truths? To understand this enigmatic book, we must peel away layers of misconception and see it for what it truly is: a message of hope, resilience, and divine love.

A Living Narrative, Not a Blueprint for the Future

Picture Revelation as a cosmic drama unfolding before your eyes. It is alive with symbolism, its scenes painted in strokes of fire, light, and shadow. Many approach this text as though it were a map, predicting precise events that will unfold in the future—a timeline of the world's end. But this interpretation misses the essence of Revelation.

Its genre, **apocalyptic literature**, is not about exact dates or literal outcomes. Instead, it reveals eternal truths about humanity's journey through the struggle toward redemption. The Seven Seals, the Four Horsemen, and the Beast are not future news headlines—they are reflections of spiritual, societal, and personal challenges that repeat throughout history.

- **Imagine this:** You're facing a period of chaos in your life, where conflict, scarcity, and fear feel insurmountable. The Four Horsemen ride not across a distant battlefield but through your own heart. Revelation's symbols become a mirror, urging you to confront your inner struggles and reminding you that these trials are part of the journey toward growth.

When we release the need for literal interpretations, the deeper message emerges: a story of **transformation**, where good triumphs over evil, not through force, but through faith and love.

Not Destruction, But Renewal

Revelation's imagery of destruction—the plagues, earthquakes, and falling stars—often overwhelms readers, painting the book as a harbinger of doom. But pause and look closer. These moments of upheaval are not the story's climax; they are its turning points.

- **Imagine a forest fire:** At first, it seems catastrophic. The flames consume everything in their path. Yet, in the ashes, seeds begin to sprout, and life returns stronger than before. Revelation's trials are like this fire, clearing the way for renewal.

The New Heaven and New Earth, introduced in the book's final chapters, is the heart of Revelation's message. It's a vision not of destruction, but of restoration—a world where pain and sorrow are no more. It promises unity, peace, and divine presence.

- **Reflection:** In your own life, what "fires" have you faced? What losses or upheavals ultimately made space for something new and beautiful? Revelation teaches us to trust that every ending carries within it the seed of renewal.

The Symbols Speak in Metaphors

Revelation is a symphony of symbols—the Beast, the Dragon, the Four Horsemen. Taken literally, these images can feel like the stuff of nightmares. But symbols are the language of the soul, meant to provoke reflection rather than fear.

- The **Beast** is not a single villain or future dictator—it represents the forces of oppression and corruption that exist in every age.
- The **Dragon** symbolizes chaos, the primal fears that threaten to undo us.

- The **Four Horsemen** are not physical riders galloping toward Earth, but representations of universal trials: conflict, scarcity, mortality, and fear.

Each symbol invites us to look inward and outward, to confront the challenges within ourselves and in the world around us.

- **Reflection:** What "beasts" do you face in your daily life? Perhaps it's fear, anger, or injustice. Revelation's symbols remind us that these forces are not insurmountable. With faith and courage, they can be overcome.

Not Just About the End Times

While Revelation is often viewed as a book about the apocalypse, its message transcends time. It speaks not only of an ultimate culmination but also of the cycles of life—struggle, transformation, and renewal—that we all experience.

- **Think of the Seven Seals:** They don't represent a single moment in history but the recurring trials that mark the human journey. Each seal opened is a lesson learned, each trial faced a step toward spiritual growth.

By focusing solely on Revelation as an "end-times" prophecy, we risk missing its relevance to our everyday lives. Its themes—faith, perseverance, and renewal—are guides for navigating modern challenges, from personal struggles to global crises.

A Message of Hope, Not Fear

Revelation begins with a powerful phrase spoken to John: **"Do not be afraid."** This is the lens through which we are meant to view the entire book. While its imagery is dramatic, its purpose is not to intimidate but to inspire awe and reverence for God's ultimate plan.

The Lamb, a central figure in Revelation, embodies humility and love. It is not through violence but through sacrifice that the Lamb triumphs. This is the book's deepest truth: love is stronger than fear, stronger than evil, stronger than death.

- **Imagine this:** You're standing in the midst of life's storms, overwhelmed by uncertainty. Revelation whispers that you are not alone. It assures you that beyond the chaos lies peace, beyond the struggle lies renewal.

A Journey Toward Transformation

Revelation isn't a riddle to solve—it's a journey to live. It invites us to see our lives mirrored in its pages, to recognize that its trials and triumphs are our own.

- When you face fear, hear the Lamb's quiet assurance: **"Do not be afraid."**
- When life feels chaotic, remember the promise of the New Jerusalem—a vision of peace that begins in your own heart.
- When you encounter the symbols of Revelation, let them guide you inward, asking,

What are they teaching me about my own journey?

A Closing Invitation

Step into Revelation not with fear but with curiosity. Let its symbols speak to you, its stories guide you, and its promises fill you with hope.

Picture yourself standing before the gates of the New Jerusalem. Its light spills out, illuminating the path ahead. In this moment, Revelation is not just a book—it is a living, breathing testament to the resilience of the human spirit and the enduring power of divine love.

Its message is clear: renewal is always within reach, and the greatest story is still unfolding—yours.

PART TWELVE

LIVING REVELATION – BRINGING THE VISION TO LIFE

Revelation is not a distant prophecy locked in the past or future—it is a living story, unfolding every day through the choices we make and the lives we lead. Its visions of renewal, justice, and divine presence call us to weave its teachings into the fabric of our daily existence. It's as if Revelation is a guide, whispering, "Step into the New Jerusalem—not someday, but now."

Practicing Resilience Through Faith

The trials of Revelation—the seals, the trumpets, and the bowls—paint a vivid picture of hardship. But as the story unfolds, it becomes clear that these challenges are not the end of the story; they are the refining fires that lead to renewal.

- **Imagine this:** You're walking through a storm. The wind lashes at you, and the path is obscured by darkness. Yet ahead, a faint light beckons. Revelation assures you that the storm is temporary and that every step through it strengthens your resolve.

Revelation's trials mirror the struggles of our lives: moments of loss, uncertainty, and fear. But in those moments, the book's wisdom invites us to find strength not in avoiding the storm, but in walking through it with faith.

- **Reflection:** When have you faced a storm in your life and come through stronger on the other side? Revelation reminds us that hardship is not the final chapter—it is a doorway to growth.

Cultivating Compassion and Justice

The New Jerusalem is a city of light and love, where diversity is celebrated, and peace reigns. It's not just a vision of the divine realm; it's a blueprint for how we can live together on earth.

- **Imagine this:** You stand at the gates of the New Jerusalem. Its golden streets are alive with laughter and kindness. People of all nations, cultures, and backgrounds gather under the Tree of Life, its leaves shimmering with the promise of healing. This is not a far-off dream—it's a call to action here and now.

Revelation urges us to cultivate inclusivity and fairness in our communities. Acts of kindness, no matter how small, become bricks in the foundation of this sacred city.

- **Action:** Volunteer at a food pantry, mentor someone in need, or simply show patience and understanding to a stranger. Every act of compassion brings the New Jerusalem closer to reality.

Embracing Stewardship of the Earth

When Revelation speaks of a New Heaven and New Earth, it's not just a promise of what's to come—it's a reminder of our responsibility to care for creation. The earth is sacred, and our stewardship reflects our reverence for the divine.

- **Picture this:** A barren field transformed into a lush garden, life bursting from the soil. Revelation's vision of renewal begins with us—each choice we make to honor and protect the earth contributes to this transformation.
- **Action:** Start small. Plant a tree, reduce waste, or participate in a community cleanup. These acts are more than environmental care; they are spiritual practices, aligning our lives with the harmony of the New Heaven and New Earth.

Building Stronger Communities

Revelation's story is not about individuals—it's about a collective journey. The New Jerusalem is a city, a symbol of unity where every person has a place and purpose.

- **Imagine this:** A community garden flourishes in the heart of a neighborhood. People from all walks of life come together to tend the soil, sharing laughter and stories. The garden is not just a source of food; it's a living metaphor for Revelation's call to collaboration and care.
- **Action:** Start or join local initiatives—whether it's a food pantry, a cultural exchange, or an interfaith dialogue. These efforts echo the inclusivity of the New Jerusalem, where every voice matters, and every hand contributes.

Personal Spiritual Practices Inspired by Revelation

Revelation is rich with imagery that invites reflection. The silence of the Seventh Seal, the serenity of the Tree of Life, and the humility of the Lamb—all these symbols encourage us to align our daily lives with divine purpose.

- **Picture this:** At the close of the day, you sit in stillness. The chaos of the world fades, replaced by the quiet wisdom of Revelation's images. You meditate on the Lamb, its quiet strength becoming your own.
- **Action:**

1. **Meditation:** Begin each day with a few minutes of reflection on a Revelation symbol. Let the Lamb inspire humility or the Tree of Life guide your commitment to healing.
2. **Journaling:** Write about challenges, triumphs, and lessons. Let Revelation's imagery prompt your entries. For example, how has a recent struggle mirrored the trials of the seals?

3. **Gratitude:** End your day by listing moments of kindness or resilience. These simple practices align your heart with the hope Revelation offers.

Fostering Global Awareness

Revelation's vision is global, and its promise for all nations and peoples. The Tree of Life's healing leaves are described as being "for the nations," emphasizing inclusivity and the interconnectedness of humanity.

- **Imagine this:** A world where borders blur, and people come together to heal wounds—cultural, environmental, and spiritual. Revelation's call for global unity begins with small steps.
- **Action:**

1. Support causes that align with Revelation's themes, such as climate action, human rights, or poverty alleviation.
2. Advocate for change by using your voice to support policies that promote justice and renewal.
3. Celebrate diversity. Attend cultural festivals, engage in interfaith dialogues, and support global arts. Each act reflects the unity of the New Jerusalem.

A Daily Call to Live Revelation

Revelation is not confined to the past or future—it calls us to live its lessons now. Imagine each day as a chapter in the unfolding story of renewal:

- **In the morning:** Reflect on a Revelation symbol and set an intention for your day. Perhaps it's humility inspired by the Lamb or healing inspired by the Tree of Life.
- **During the day,** Look for ways to embody compassion and justice, whether in small acts of kindness or larger advocacy efforts.

- **In the evening:** Reflect on how your actions brought light into the world, and offer gratitude for the chance to be part of Revelation's vision.

A Final Invitation

Revelation is a book of transformation, but it is also a call—a call to live with courage, hope, and purpose. Imagine yourself walking through the New Jerusalem, its streets golden with possibility. Each step you take brings you closer to its light.

You are not just a reader of Revelation; you are a participant in its unfolding story. With every act of kindness, every moment of reflection, and every effort to build a just and compassionate world, you bring its vision to life.

Revelation whispers: **The New Jerusalem is not far away—it begins with you.**

PART THIRTEEN

PROPHECY, VISION, AND MODERN APPLICATION

Revelation, with its vivid prophecies and transcendent visions, speaks across the ages. It is not confined to a distant past or a far-off future—it is alive, a guide for navigating the complexities of today's world. Each symbol, each prophecy, holds a mirror to the challenges we face and offers a pathway forward. What if Revelation is not merely a text to be studied but a story to be lived? What if its lessons are an invitation to transform ourselves and the world around us?

Prophecy as a Call to Action: Hearing the Trumpets of Change

The sound of a trumpet in Revelation is a summons, a wake-up call echoing through time. These prophetic moments—whether in the opening of the seals or the blowing of the trumpets—aren't meant to induce fear but to stir us into action.

- **Picture this:** You're standing on a hillside at dawn. A trumpet blast cuts through the stillness, its sound reverberating in your chest. It's a call to wake up, to rise, and to act. Revelation's prophecies are like that trumpet, urging us to reflect on the state of our hearts and the world.

These warnings challenge us to confront personal and societal failures, not with despair, but with resolve. They invite us to ask hard questions:

- Where am I complicit in systems of injustice?
- How can I align my life more fully with love and integrity?
- What actions can I take to heal the wounds of my community?

Modern Application:

- Advocate for social justice, addressing inequalities in education, healthcare, or housing.
- Reflect on your spiritual journey—what needs to be refined, strengthened, or let go?

- Support movements that promote reconciliation and peace, standing as a witness for change.

The New Jerusalem: A Vision of Harmony and Renewal

Revelation's New Jerusalem glimmers on the horizon of the text—a city of light, unity, and peace. But this vision isn't meant to stay on the page; it's a blueprint for the world we can build.

- **Imagine this:** You walk through the gates of the New Jerusalem. Its golden streets radiate warmth, not from wealth, but from the shared kindness of its people. Its walls embrace diversity, and its air hums with the music of healing and reconciliation.

This vision challenges us to rethink our priorities. It asks us to create communities where no one is excluded, where decisions are made with wisdom and compassion, and where the Earth itself is cherished as sacred.

Modern Application:

- **Environmental Sustainability:** Begin with small steps—reduce waste, plant trees, or advocate for renewable energy. The New Jerusalem's harmony starts with how we treat our planet.
- **Inclusive Governance:** Work toward equitable policies in your local government, school board, or workplace. Ensure every voice is heard.
- **Healing and Reconciliation:** Support programs that mend divides, whether racial, cultural, or interfaith. Create spaces where understanding can flourish.

Revelation's Symbols: Guides for Modern Life

The symbols of Revelation are like stars in a night sky—distant, yet luminous, guiding us toward deeper truths.

- **The Lamb:** The Lamb's gentle power shows us that leadership doesn't require domination but humility and sacrificial love.

- **Application:** In your workplace or community, lead with compassion. Volunteer time and resources for the vulnerable. The Lamb's way is one of lifting others up.
- **The Tree of Life:** Its leaves are for the healing of nations—a call to nurture renewal and wholeness.
- **Application:** Support mental health initiatives, advocate for accessible healthcare, or plant trees in your neighborhood. Healing begins with care.
- **The Four Horsemen:** They represent the trials of life—conflict, scarcity, and mortality—but also invite resilience and response.
- **Application:** Confront these challenges with action. Advocate for peace, combat hunger through donations or service, and support global health efforts.

Collective Movements: Uniting for Transformation

Revelation's global scale reminds us that some challenges can only be met together. Its visions of nations gathering in the light of the Tree of Life inspire us to collaborate across boundaries.

Imagine this: A world where people come together—not driven by fear, but united by a shared commitment to justice, stewardship, and renewal. This is Revelation's dream—a dream we can make real.

Modern Application:

- Join climate action groups, recognizing that environmental stewardship is a collective effort.
- Support interfaith initiatives that foster understanding and unity among diverse communities.
- Stand with advocacy campaigns that address systemic inequality, from poverty to racial injustice.

Personal Reflection: Prophecy as a Mirror

Revelation's prophecies aren't just about the world—they're about us. They challenge us to look inward, to examine our hearts, and to align our lives with divine purpose.

- **Picture this:** You sit in a quiet room, Revelation's words before you. As you read, it feels as though a mirror is being held up to your soul. The questions come: What fears hold me back? What habits need to change? What dreams am I called to pursue?

Prophecy is not a prediction of inevitable doom; it's an invitation to transformation. It asks us to step into a new way of being—one marked by courage, integrity, and faith.

Modern Application:

- Set aside time each week for reflection. Use journaling or guided meditation to explore how Revelation's themes resonate in your life.
- Identify one area of your life—relationships, work, faith—where you feel called to grow. Take small, intentional steps toward change.

A Call to Live Revelation

Revelation is not a distant story—it unfolds in every moment, inviting us to join in its vision of renewal and hope.

- **In your daily life:** Start each morning with a simple question: **How can I bring light into the world today?** Let Revelation's symbols—like the Lamb or the Tree of Life—guide your actions.
- **In your community:** Look for ways to foster unity, justice, and healing. Whether through volunteering, mentoring, or organizing, every effort becomes a reflection of the New Jerusalem.
- **In the world:** Support movements that echo Revelation's call for stewardship, justice, and peace. Your voice and actions matter.

A Vision of Renewal

Revelation's promise is clear: even in the face of trials, there is hope. Even amid chaos, there is the potential for renewal. The New Jerusalem isn't a distant dream—it's a call to action.

- **Imagine this:** The gates of the city are open, its light spilling into the world. You are walking toward it, not alone, but with others. Each step is a prayer, a promise, a declaration of faith. Together, you are building a world that reflects the divine harmony Revelation envisions.

Let Revelation's words inspire your journey. Let its visions shape your actions. And let its hope carry you forward, knowing that even the smallest step toward renewal is part of a greater story—one written by love, justice, and grace.

PART FOURTEEN

REVELATION AND PERSONAL TRANSFORMATION

Revelation, often viewed as a book of prophecy and cosmic drama, holds within its pages a deeply personal message: the power of transformation. Beyond its apocalyptic imagery lies a guide for spiritual growth and renewal, a roadmap for individuals seeking to align their lives with divine purpose. Revelation isn't just a vision of the world's future—it's an invitation to reimagine your own life, to see every challenge as a step toward personal transformation.

In this chapter, we'll delve into how Revelation's symbols, lessons, and themes can inspire your journey of faith and provide tools for self-discovery, spiritual alignment, and purposeful living.

Engaging Revelation Through Practical Exercises

Revelation's imagery and lessons come alive when we actively engage with them. By integrating its symbols and messages into daily life, you can uncover profound insights about your spiritual path.

Journaling Prompts: A Path to Inner Clarity

Journaling is a powerful way to reflect on Revelation's teachings and their relevance to your life. Consider these prompts to guide your writing:

- **The Tree of Life (Revelation 22:2):** What nourishes your spiritual journey? How do you cultivate growth and healing in your life and relationships?
- **The Lamb (Revelation 5:6):** How does the Lamb's example of sacrifice and victory inspire you to overcome challenges and serve others?

- **The New Jerusalem (Revelation 21):** What areas of your life need renewal? How can you bring harmony and peace into your interactions and decisions?

Meditative Practices: Encountering Revelation's Symbols

Meditation offers a way to internalize Revelation's imagery and connect with its spiritual truths.

- **Visualize the River of Life:** Close your eyes and imagine standing by a river that flows from the throne of God. Picture its waters bringing renewal and clarity to every aspect of your life.
- **Focus on a Weekly Symbol:** Choose one symbol—such as the Gates of the New Jerusalem or the Tree of Life—and meditate on its meaning. How does it speak to your current challenges or aspirations?

The Role of Symbols in Self-Discovery

Revelation's symbols are not just artistic flourishes; they are keys to understanding the deeper truths of your spiritual journey. They offer a unique language for exploring your inner self and aligning with divine purpose.

The Tree of Life: Growth and Nourishment

The Tree of Life symbolizes healing, growth, and connection to the divine. Its roots reach deep, drawing nourishment, while its leaves extend outward, offering healing to all.

- **Exercise:** Draw or visualize your own Tree of Life. What are the roots that ground you—family, faith, or personal values? What branches represent your aspirations, and what fruits reflect your accomplishments?

The Lamb: Sacrifice and Victory

The Lamb, a central figure in Revelation, embodies humility, redemption, and triumph through sacrifice.

- **Exercise:** Reflect on moments when you have faced challenges and emerged stronger through faith. What sacrifices have you made that led to growth, and how can you carry the Lamb's qualities into your daily actions?

The New Jerusalem: Renewal and Harmony

The New Jerusalem, with its gates open to all nations, symbolizes ultimate peace and unity.

- **Exercise:** Identify areas of your life in need of renewal—relationships, career, or personal habits. What practical steps can you take to bring harmony and alignment to these areas?

Developing a Personal Connection to Revelation

Revelation invites a deep, personal engagement with its teachings. By connecting its themes to your own experiences, you can make its messages a living part of your journey.

Daily Affirmations: Aligning With Revelation's Vision

Start your day with affirmations inspired by Revelation's themes:

- "I walk a path of renewal, guided by divine wisdom."
- "Challenges are opportunities for transformation, and I embrace them with faith."

Spiritual Rituals: Bringing Revelation to Life

Create meaningful rituals that connect you to Revelation's messages:

- **Lighting a Candle:** While reading passages from Revelation, light a candle to symbolize the light of hope and faith guiding you through life's darkness.
- **Writing to Your Future Self:** Pen a letter to yourself inspired by Revelation's vision of renewal, detailing the person you hope to become and the steps you will take to get there.

Revelation's Call to Transformation: A Journey of Renewal

At its heart, Revelation is a story of transformation—of a world renewed, of hearts mended, of light triumphing over darkness. Its lessons inspire personal growth that ripples outward, touching every aspect of life.

Practical Actions for Living Revelation

- **Volunteer in Your Community:** Embody the principles of justice and renewal by participating in projects that serve the vulnerable or protect the environment.
- **Cultivate Daily Habits of Peace:** Practice gratitude, engage in acts of kindness, and learn the art of conflict resolution to foster harmony in your relationships.

Living a Life of Purpose

Revelation reminds us that every challenge we face is an opportunity to grow spiritually and align with divine purpose. When you view life through its lens, even ordinary moments become part of an extraordinary journey.

A Framework for Spiritual Growth

Revelation provides a profound framework for personal transformation, offering tools for reflection and growth:

1. **Resilience:** Its trials teach us that hardship is not an end but a pathway to greater strength and clarity.
2. **Hope:** Its vision of the New Jerusalem assures us that renewal is always possible, no matter how dire the circumstances.
3. **Alignment:** Its symbols guide us to live in harmony with divine principles of love, justice, and unity.

A Final Invitation: Your Journey of Renewal

Close your eyes and imagine yourself stepping into Revelation's story. You are walking along the River of Life, its waters shimmering with light. In the distance, the Tree of Life spreads its branches, offering shade and healing. The gates of the New Jerusalem stand open, welcoming you into a realm of peace and possibility.

This isn't just a vision—it's your life, here and now. Each step you take toward personal transformation, every effort to bring renewal and harmony into the world, is part of this unfolding story.

Let Revelation inspire you to live fully, to embrace challenges as opportunities for growth, and to act courageously in the face of uncertainty. Its promise is clear: renewal is within reach, and transformation begins with you.

You are not just a reader of Revelation—you are its living reflection. Step into its light, and let its vision guide your path.

PART FIFTEEN

THE ROLE OF WOMEN IN REVELATION

Women play significant roles in Revelation, symbolizing pivotal themes of spiritual transformation, resilience, and divine justice. Through figures such as the Woman Clothed with the Sun and the Scarlet Woman, Revelation uses feminine imagery to convey profound truths. This section delves into these portrayals, exploring their meanings and implications for spiritual growth and understanding.

1. The Woman Clothed with the Sun

- **Biblical Description**: Found in Revelation 12, this figure is adorned with the sun, standing on the moon, and crowned with twelve stars. She is in labor, bringing forth a child who is destined to rule all nations.
    - **Symbolism**:
        - The Woman represents the divine feminine, the church, or Israel, embodying purity, endurance, and divine purpose.
        - Her child symbolizes Christ or the emergence of divine truth and justice.
- **Spiritual Implications**:
    - The image of the Woman highlights the struggles and triumphs of bringing spiritual truth into a world of opposition.
    - **Reflection**: Consider the ways in which challenges in your life serve as a birthing process for new spiritual insights or actions.

2. The Scarlet Woman

- **Biblical Description**: Revelation 17 introduces the Scarlet Woman, seated on a beast and adorned in purple and scarlet, holding a golden cup filled with abominations.
    - **Symbolism**:

        - Often interpreted as a representation of corrupt systems or false religion.
        - The beast she rides symbolizes oppressive power.
- **Spiritual Implications**:
    - The Scarlet Woman serves as a cautionary figure, urging readers to discern and resist forces that lead away from spiritual truth.
    - **Reflection**: Identify areas in life where materialism or corrupt influences may be overshadowing spiritual values.

3. Feminine Archetypes and Their Lessons

Revelation's use of feminine imagery reflects universal archetypes of creation, transformation, and resilience.

- **The Divine Feminine:**
    - Embodied by the Woman Clothed with the Sun, representing nurture, protection, and divine purpose.
    - Lesson: Embrace qualities of care and endurance in your spiritual journey.
- **The Shadow Feminine:**
    - Represented by the Scarlet Woman, highlighting the dangers of imbalance and material excess.
    - Lesson: Cultivate discernment to navigate life's challenges with wisdom and integrity.

4. The Role of Women in Modern Application

Revelation's feminine imagery offers valuable lessons for modern readers, both men and women.

- **Empowerment Through Struggle:**
    - Like the Woman Clothed with the Sun, individuals can find strength and purpose through challenges.
    - Action Step: Reflect on a personal struggle and identify the growth or transformation it has brought.

- **Discernment and Resistance:**
  - The Scarlet Woman's cautionary tale encourages vigilance against forces that undermine spiritual integrity.
  - Action Step: Examine areas where external pressures may conflict with inner spiritual values.

Conclusion: Women as Catalysts for Transformation

In Revelation, women symbolize both the potential for divine renewal and the pitfalls of spiritual deviation. Their roles invite readers to reflect on their own spiritual journeys, emphasizing endurance, discernment, and transformation. By understanding these archetypes, individuals can embrace the divine feminine within themselves, fostering balance, resilience, and a deeper connection to the eternal truths of Revelation.

PART SIXTEEN

REVELATION AND ENVIRONMENTAL STEWARDSHIP

Revelation is a book of renewal, where nature is not only the backdrop of divine action but an integral part of the story. Its vivid imagery reveals the Earth as a creation of divine beauty, brimming with potential for restoration. Far from being disposable, the world is shown as a sacred trust—a masterpiece that reflects the Creator's love. In its final chapters, Revelation invites us to reimagine the relationship between humanity and the environment, presenting a vision where stewardship and restoration lead to the flourishing of all creation.

This chapter delves into Revelation's ecological themes, exploring how they inspire a call to action. By aligning our care for the Earth with Revelation's vision, we step into a divine narrative where environmental stewardship becomes a spiritual practice and a moral responsibility.

Ecological Themes in Revelation: A Vision of Renewal

Nature flows through Revelation like a current, from the River of Life to the New Heaven and New Earth. These symbols are not mere poetic flourishes; they are declarations of hope and renewal, rooted in the interconnectedness of all creation.

The New Heaven and New Earth: Creation Renewed

In Revelation 21:1, John sees a vision of a New Heaven and New Earth, unblemished and free from decay. This moment signifies the ultimate redemption of creation, where the scars of exploitation and corruption are healed.

- **Reflection:** What would it mean to see the Earth as sacred and capable of renewal? Imagine a world where the rivers run clean, forests thrive, and all living creatures flourish. This vision is not distant—it begins with the choices we make today.

The River of Life and the Tree of Life: Nature's Healing Power

In Revelation 22:1-2, the River of Life flows clear and pure, nourishing the Tree of Life, whose leaves bring healing to the nations. This imagery reminds us that nature itself is a gift, a source of sustenance and restoration.

- **Lesson:** The health of the Earth and the health of our spirits are intertwined. When we care for creation, we participate in God's sustaining work. Neglecting the environment is not only a practical failure but a spiritual one.

Humanity's Role as Stewards of Creation

From the first pages of the Bible to the last, humanity's role as stewards of the Earth is a central theme. Revelation completes the story begun in Genesis, showing how our stewardship fulfills God's design for creation.

Biblical Foundations: A Sacred Mandate

In Genesis 2:15, humanity is placed in the garden to "tend and keep it." This charge is not about domination but care—ensuring that creation thrives. Revelation 21 and 22 show the fulfillment of this mandate, where stewardship leads to the flourishing of a renewed creation.

- **Insight:** Stewardship is not an optional task; it is a divine calling. To care for the Earth is to honor the Creator. When we neglect this responsibility, we stray from our spiritual purpose.

Modern Implications: Living the Mandate Today

In today's world, stewardship takes on urgent significance. Climate change, deforestation, and pollution are not just ecological crises but moral challenges. Revelation's vision compels us to act:

- Reduce waste and energy consumption.
- Support environmental justice, ensuring vulnerable communities are not disproportionately harmed by ecological neglect.
- Advocate for renewable energy and policies that prioritize sustainability.

Practical Applications for Environmental Stewardship

Revelation's call to renewal invites us to transform our care for the Earth into daily practices and collective efforts.

Daily Actions: Small Steps, Big Impact

- Reduce single-use plastics, conserve water, and minimize energy consumption.
- Choose sustainable products and support companies that prioritize environmental responsibility.
- Compost and recycle to reduce landfill waste.

Community Initiatives: A Shared Responsibility

- **Tree-Planting Events:** Organize or participate in tree-planting drives, symbolizing growth and renewal.
- **Clean-Up Campaigns:** Collaborate with neighbors to clean rivers, parks, or neighborhoods, reflecting the vision of a pristine New Heaven and New Earth.
- **Educational Workshops:** Host workshops on sustainable living, teaching others about composting, energy conservation, and renewable resources.

Revelation's Vision as Motivation for Change

Revelation doesn't just highlight the beauty of a renewed creation—it calls us to act with hope and accountability.

Hope Through Renewal

The promise of a New Heaven and New Earth reminds us that restoration is always possible. Even in the face of climate challenges, Revelation inspires action rather than despair.

- **Reflection:** How does hope motivate your care for the Earth? Instead of being overwhelmed by the scale of environmental issues, focus on the small changes that, collectively, lead to renewal.

Spiritual Accountability

Revelation challenges us to align our actions with divine principles. Caring for creation is not separate from faith—it is an expression of it. Every effort to protect the Earth reflects our commitment to God's design.

Connection to Modern Environmental Movements

Revelation's themes resonate with contemporary movements that link spirituality and ecological care.

Climate Change Awareness

Revelation's warnings of catastrophic events echo the consequences of environmental neglect. Droughts, wildfires, and rising sea levels are stark reminders of the fragility of creation.

- **Insight:** Revelation invites us to respond to these challenges not with fear but with determination, working to reverse ecological damage and prevent further harm.

Global and Local Activism

Communities inspired by Revelation can contribute to environmental movements on multiple levels:

- **Grassroots Efforts:** Participate in local initiatives like community gardens or clean-up drives.

- **Global Advocacy:** Support organizations like "Green Faith," which integrate ecological stewardship with spiritual practice.
- **Policy Change:** Advocate for laws that promote sustainability, protect natural habitats, and address climate justice.

Revelation as a Call to Ecological Renewal

Revelation's vision of a renewed Earth is both a promise and a challenge. It assures us that restoration is possible but also reminds us that this vision requires action. Caring for creation is not just about preserving beauty—it's about aligning with divine intention.

A Sacred Responsibility

Imagine the Earth as a garden, entrusted to us by God. Its rivers, forests, and skies are gifts meant to be cherished, not exploited. Every tree we plant, every habitat we protect, is an act of worship—a reflection of our gratitude for creation.

A Shared Journey

Environmental stewardship is not a solitary effort; it is a collective calling. Communities working together to care for the Earth embody the unity and hope of the New Jerusalem.

A Final Reflection: Living the Vision of Renewal

Close your eyes and picture the River of Life, its waters clear and sparkling. Imagine the Tree of Life, its leaves offering healing to all nations. This isn't just a vision of the future—it's a blueprint for how we can live today.

Revelation calls us to be stewards of this sacred creation, to align our actions with its promise of renewal. Let this vision inspire you to act with purpose and to care for the Earth not only as a duty but as a joy. Together, we can ensure that the beauty and balance of creation endure for generations to come.

Practical Takeaways

1. Start small: Reduce waste, conserve energy, and plant trees.
2. Join community initiatives: Advocate for environmental justice and support clean-up projects.
3. Reflect spiritually: See environmental stewardship as an expression of faith and gratitude.

Revelation offers not just a promise of renewal but a call to action. The Earth's future is in our hands—let us care for it as stewards of divine creation.

PART SEVENTEEN

REVELATION AND THE POWER OF COMMUNITY

Revelation is not merely a story of personal transformation—it is a profound call to unity, collaboration, and shared purpose. It speaks to the heart of what it means to be part of something greater, a thread in the vast tapestry of humanity and divinity. The text reminds us that transformation is not a solitary journey; it unfolds most fully in the context of community. Revelation paints a vivid picture of a world where individuals come together, transcending barriers of culture, language, and history, to create a harmonious whole.

This chapter explores how Revelation inspires the formation of compassionate, justice-driven communities and offers a roadmap for applying its teachings to the challenges of modern societal structures.

Revelation's Vision of Community

At its heart, Revelation offers a vision of unity and collective purpose that is as urgent today as it was when John first penned his words.

The New Jerusalem: A Model of Unity

In Revelation 21, we are introduced to the **New Jerusalem**, a city of light and peace where all nations gather under God's guidance. Its gates are always open, welcoming everyone without distinction.

- **Reflection:** Imagine a community where every person is valued, where diversity is celebrated, and where shared goals take precedence over divisions. The New Jerusalem is not just a vision for the future—it is an invitation to create such a community here and now.
- **Insight:** The New Jerusalem's inclusivity challenges us to break down barriers of race, religion, and culture, fostering

relationships rooted in mutual respect and understanding. It calls us to build communities that reflect divine harmony and justice.

The Multitude in White Robes: Unity in Diversity

In Revelation 7:9, John sees a great multitude "from every nation, tribe, people, and language" standing before the throne, united in worship. This scene is a powerful image of diversity embraced under a common purpose.

- **Lesson:** Revelation celebrates the richness of human diversity while reminding us of our shared humanity. It invites us to see our differences not as divisions but as expressions of the Creator's infinite creativity.
- **Reflection Question:** How can your community embrace its diversity while working toward shared spiritual or societal goals?

Lessons for Modern Communities

Revelation's teachings offer timeless lessons for building communities that embody compassion, justice, and unity.

Inclusivity and Compassion: Welcoming All

Revelation's vision of open gates and diverse multitudes highlights the importance of inclusivity. In a world often fractured by prejudice, this is a radical call to create spaces where everyone feels welcome.

Practical Application:

- Create opportunities for dialogue across differences, such as interfaith gatherings or cultural festivals.
- Establish safe spaces where marginalized voices are heard and celebrated.

Justice and Advocacy: Standing Against Oppression

Throughout Revelation, oppressive systems are exposed and condemned, from Babylon's decadence to the Beast's tyranny. This imagery calls us to challenge systems of injustice in our own time.

Practical Application:

- Support initiatives addressing poverty, inequality, and environmental degradation.
- Advocate for policies that promote equity and sustainability.
- **Insight:** Justice is not a passive hope—it is an active pursuit. Revelation reminds us that communities thrive when they work together to dismantle oppression and build structures of fairness and care.

Building Revelation-Inspired Communities

The vision of Revelation isn't just an abstract ideal; it is a blueprint for action. By drawing on its themes, we can create communities that reflect its principles of renewal and hope.

Faith-Based Collaboration: Finding Common Ground

Revelation shows that unity is possible even in diversity. Its vision encourages communities to come together around shared values.

- **Action Step:** Organize events that bring people of different faiths and cultures together to discuss common goals, such as environmental care or social justice. These collaborations reflect the unity of the New Jerusalem.

Acts of Service: Faith in Action

Revelation emphasizes that faith must be lived out through service. The Lamb's humility and sacrifice are models for how we can serve others.

Action Step:

- Participate in food drives, disaster relief efforts, or mentorship programs.
- Volunteer in projects that address both immediate needs and long-term solutions, such as literacy programs or sustainable agriculture initiatives.

Celebrating Together: Collective Gratitude

Revelation is filled with imagery of worship and celebration, reminding us of the joy that comes from shared spiritual practices.

- **Action Step:** Host events centered on gratitude, renewal, and unity, such as community meals, interfaith worship services, or music and arts festivals.

Sustaining Community Bonds

Creating a Revelation-inspired community is not a one-time effort; it requires ongoing reflection, renewal, and collaboration.

Regular Reflection and Renewal

Communities flourish when they reconnect with their shared mission. Revelation's cycles of judgment and renewal mirror the need for communities to regularly assess their purpose and progress.

- **Practical Tip:** Hold periodic retreats or meetings where members can reflect on their goals and recommit to their shared vision.

Intergenerational Collaboration

Revelation emphasizes the importance of legacy, showing how continuity sustains hope. Communities thrive when wisdom is passed down and younger generations are empowered to lead.

Action Step:

- Create mentorship programs where older members share their experiences and younger members bring fresh energy and ideas.
- Celebrate milestones together, fostering a sense of shared history and purpose.

Revelation's Call to Community: A Unified Vision

Revelation challenges us to think beyond ourselves and to embrace the power of collective action and shared purpose. Its vision of the New Jerusalem is not just an endpoint—it is a way of life.

A Community of Hope

Imagine a world where people work together to heal wounds, foster understanding, and build a just society. This is the promise of Revelation's vision.

A Community of Action

Every small step—whether planting a tree, mentoring a child, or hosting a dialogue—reflects the light of the New Jerusalem. These acts, multiplied by many hands, create a legacy of love and renewal.

A Final Reflection: Building the New Jerusalem

Close your eyes and picture yourself walking through the gates of the New Jerusalem. You see people from every background, their differences woven into a beautiful tapestry. You hear laughter, songs, and prayers—expressions of gratitude and hope.

This is the community Revelation invites us to create. It begins with you and the circles you touch. By fostering inclusivity, pursuing justice, and celebrating unity, you can help build a world that reflects the eternal truths of Revelation.

Let the power of community guide you. Let its vision inspire your actions. Together, we can create spaces where hope flourishes, justice prevails, and love binds us as one.

PART EIGHTEEN

REVELATION'S TIMELESS LESSONS FOR MODERN CHALLENGES

The Book of Revelation is not a mere chronicle of apocalyptic visions; it is a timeless guide for enduring hope, transformation, and action. While its vivid imagery and prophetic tone are rooted in an ancient context, its lessons resonate across generations, offering profound wisdom for the complexities of modern life. Revelation dares us to see beyond the chaos of the present, illuminating a path toward justice, renewal, and unity.

In a world grappling with profound challenges—pandemics, climate change, social inequity, and political unrest—Revelation serves as both a mirror and a map. It reflects humanity's struggles while charting a way forward, inviting us to align our lives with its call for divine harmony and collective restoration.

A Message of Faith Amidst Uncertainty

Revelation unfolds in a world shaken by upheaval—its scenes of cosmic disturbances and tribulation mirror the unpredictability of our own time. Yet within this turmoil, Revelation speaks a deeper truth: that faith is not an escape from hardship but a foundation for resilience.

The Call to Endure

The trials depicted in Revelation—the opening of the seals, the sounding of the trumpets, and the pouring of the bowls—are not endpoints but catalysts for transformation. They symbolize the challenges that test the human spirit, ultimately leading to renewal.

- **Reflection:** How do we face the "seals" of our own lives? Whether through personal struggles or global crises, Revelation reminds us that these moments of difficulty are opportunities for growth and alignment with divine purpose.

Practical Steps to Build Resilience

- **Rituals of Grounding:** Light a candle at the end of each day, letting its flame symbolize hope amidst darkness.
- **Meditative Practices:** Reflect on Revelation's imagery, such as the River of Life or the Tree of Life, to center your thoughts and inspire renewal.
- **Acts of Kindness:** Embody the abundance of the New Jerusalem by contributing to food drives, shelters, or community aid efforts. These actions transform faith into tangible care.
- **Strengthen Community Bonds:** Join or form support networks where mutual care and shared purpose provide strength during challenging times.

Justice and Advocacy: Confronting Modern Babylons

Revelation's condemnation of Babylon—a symbol of greed, corruption, and systemic oppression—is a clarion call to confront the injustices of our time. Its imagery challenges us to identify and dismantle the "Babylons" that perpetuate harm in our world.

Recognizing Modern Babylons

Today, Babylon manifests in many forms: exploitative economic systems, environmental degradation, and inequitable policies. Revelation demands that we oppose these structures and work to create a society rooted in equity and divine principles.

- **Reflection Question:** What systems in your life or community uphold inequality or harm? How can you act as an agent of change?

Actionable Steps for Justice

- **Advocacy for Equity:** Campaign for policies that promote affordable housing, universal healthcare, and sustainable development.
- **Grassroots Engagement:** Support local initiatives addressing inequality, such as community justice programs, education reform, or climate action movements.
- **Amplify Marginalized Voices:** Create platforms for underrepresented communities, ensuring that all perspectives are valued and heard.

Embracing Renewal: Personal and Collective Transformation

Revelation's vision of a New Heaven and New Earth is a profound call to embrace renewal—not only on a global scale but within our own lives. It invites us to let go of outdated patterns and actively participate in creating a world aligned with divine purpose.

Personal Renewal: The Inner Work

Revelation challenges us to examine our inner worlds, identifying areas in need of transformation.

- **Reflection:** What habits, beliefs, or relationships no longer serve your growth? What steps can you take to welcome renewal into your life?

Collective Renewal: Building a Just Society

Revelation's vision inspires initiatives that address societal brokenness and foster reconciliation.

Practical Actions:

- Participate in projects like neighborhood revitalization, community clean-ups, or local food programs.
- Advocate for policies that protect natural resources, promote clean energy, and sustain the environment.

- Foster understanding by building bridges across cultural, ideological, and religious divides.

Hope as the Guiding Light

Hope is the heart of Revelation. Despite its depictions of tribulation, the text concludes with a triumphant vision of the New Jerusalem—a place of unity, renewal, and divine presence. This hope is not passive; it is a call to action, urging us to live as co-creators of this promised harmony.

Living With Hope

In Revelation, hope is deeply entwined with purpose. It transforms despair into courage, inspiring individuals to reflect its principles in their daily lives.

- **Acts of Renewal:** Simple gestures—planting a tree, offering a helping hand, or showing compassion—ripple outward, embodying the promise of the New Jerusalem.
- **Mindful Practices:** Begin each day with affirmations such as "I am part of a story of renewal" or "Hope guides my actions."

Revelation as a Map for Today

Revelation is not confined to the past or a distant future—it is a guide for navigating the complexities of the present. Its themes of justice, resilience, and renewal challenge us to rise above fear and uncertainty, living with intention and purpose.

Personal Transformation

- **Journaling Prompts:** Explore questions like, "What does the New Jerusalem symbolize in my life?" or "How can I reflect Revelation's call for renewal in my actions today?"
- **Mindful Alignment:** Use Revelation's teachings to inform decisions and priorities, cultivating love, resilience, and hope.

Collective Action

- **Community Engagement:** Organize events like interfaith dialogues, environmental restoration efforts, or justice-focused workshops.
- **Global Advocacy:** Join movements addressing climate change, poverty, and human rights, contributing to a collective vision of equity and peace.

Building the New Jerusalem Together

Revelation's ultimate vision—a harmonious world where nations gather in peace and creation thrives—is both a divine promise and a challenge. It calls us to act with compassion, pursue justice, and nurture hope in our choices today.

A Final Reflection

Imagine walking through the gates of the New Jerusalem. Its streets are filled with laughter, its waters flow with life, and its trees offer healing. This vision begins with us—with every act of kindness, every step toward justice, and every effort to nurture harmony in our lives and communities.

The Journey Ahead

Revelation invites us to co-create its vision, turning its timeless lessons into tangible realities. By embracing its call, we transform personal and collective challenges into opportunities for renewal, building a legacy of love, justice, and hope that will resonate for generations.

Let Revelation inspire you to live boldly, act with purpose, and walk forward as a steward of its eternal message. Together, we can bring the vision of the New Jerusalem closer to our world today.

PART NINETEEN

BUILDING LASTING LEGACIES OF FAITH AND ACTION

Revelation inspires us to create lasting legacies that offer both personal transformation and collective betterment. Establishing lasting contributions and advocating for systemic change ensure that Revelation's teachings resonate through generations.

Establishing a Legacy Project

A legacy project aligns personal values with actions that create meaningful, enduring impact. Inspired by Revelation's vision of renewal and justice, these projects bring divine principles to life:

- **Community Initiatives**: Create a local project such as a community garden, which symbolizes growth and unity, or a literacy program to empower the next generation through education.
- **Spiritual Traditions**: Establish annual events like a day of service inspired by Revelation's teachings. Encourage participation from diverse groups to promote inclusivity.
- **Philanthropic Efforts**: Start a scholarship fund for underprivileged youth or donate to causes aligned with justice and compassion, reflecting Revelation's call for equity.
- **Creative Contributions**: Use art, writing, or music to immortalize Revelation's teachings. A public mural or a book club centered around its themes fosters dialogue and understanding.

These projects ensure that Revelation's values are woven into the fabric of society, offering hope and inspiration to future generations.

Advocating for Systemic Change

Revelation's message of unity and justice calls us to address the broader systems that shape our world. Advocacy for systemic change is essential for creating a society that reflects divine harmony:

- **Social Justice Movements**: Support initiatives addressing racial, gender, and economic inequities. Volunteer with organizations that promote equity and inclusion, or participate in peaceful demonstrations.
- **Environmental Action**: Advocate for policies that combat climate change, protect natural resources, and promote sustainability. Join efforts such as reforestation campaigns or zero-waste initiatives.
- **Policy Engagement**: Work to influence local, national, or global policies that align with Revelation's vision of renewal and fairness. This could include campaigning for education reform or healthcare access.
- **Empowering Voices**: Use your platform to amplify the voices of marginalized groups, ensuring that everyone's experiences and perspectives are valued.

Advocating for systemic change transforms Revelation's call for justice into tangible actions that uplift humanity and create a world more aligned with its divine promise.

The Impact of Legacy and Advocacy

By combining personal legacy projects with systemic advocacy, we embody Revelation's teachings in profound ways. These efforts not only bring hope and renewal but also set a foundation for continued growth and unity. They encourage others to see their lives as part of a greater divine story, inspiring collective transformation for the betterment of all.

Bringing It All Together

Revelation is more than a sacred text—it is a living guide that calls us to be stewards of hope, agents of renewal, and builders of unity. By bringing its teachings to life through personal practices, community engagement, and global action, we can transform its profound messages into real-world impact.

Let Revelation inspire you to act with purpose, live with compassion, and contribute to a world that reflects its eternal promise of love and harmony.

www.ingramcontent.com/pod-product-compliance
Lightning Source LLC
LaVergne TN
LVHW010933110826
845149LV00013B/2580

* 9 7 9 8 9 9 2 1 6 6 9 8 9 *